HOW TO BOOST YOUR PROPERTY PORTFOLIO THE SMART WAY

HOW TO BOOST YOUR PROPERTY PORTFOLIO THE SMART WAY

Includes essential tools to boost your property portfolio, adapt for the changing market, protect and sustain your investments, improve your buying, letting and selling strengths and more for the smart property investor.

DANIELE STEED

authorHOUSE®

AuthorHouse™
1663 Liberty Drive
Bloomington, IN 47403
www.authorhouse.com
Phone: 1-800-839-8640

The information in this book is for educational purposes only. The content, estimates, figures and indications contained in this book are based on opinion. The author is not qualified to give any financial and legal advice, and will not accept any liability for decisions made on the content. The contents do not constitute financial advice in any way. You should seek independent professional advice before making any investment decision. Investing in property can be a risky business just like any other investment. Historical growth does not necessarily mean that prices will increase in the future. Your property may be repossessed if you do not keep up payment on your mortgage.

Published by AuthorHouse   03/12/2013

ISBN: 978-1-4817-8652-2 (sc)
ISBN: 978-1-4817-8653-9 (e)

This book is printed on acid-free paper.

Thank you to my dear Mama and Papa for their encouragement.

CONTENTS

CONVENTIONAL
VS.
CREATIVE FINANCE

Think Like A Successful Property Investor

Most of us know the true reality of the rat race, when we all see each rat rushes to catch the trains, buses or try to beat the rush hour traffic in a car to get to work on time. They fear if they are late on numerous times, or fail to meet expectations in work, or a company needs to cut jobs, they worry about losing their jobs. Job is the most taxed form of income, as much as up to 50% for specific professions and generally they are paid to completely conform to when they work, what time until when, amount in wages, even what you wear and many more. Why do you think people hate Mondays so much and can't wait for the weekend to come? I was also one of the rats who were academically trained to work for many years in the rat race until retirement, but I knew there must be more than this one choice. I enjoy working, but waiting for payday and for a set amount was like being lured to the cheese like a mouse towards the monthly mousetrap. Many of these rats can't imagine ever living a better life without a job, but to the rats, facts didn't matter. Rather than investigate and learn what alternatives exist for them, the rats all rush and cram onto the hamster wheel of the rat race and spread the fears to others that a job is the be all or end all.

All of us know people who are like the hurried and conforming rat. And, if we're honest, we all have an inner Rat fear that appears in the face of doubt and challenge.

Ultimately, if unchecked, our inner rat fear turns into cynics who always see danger and never take action. Therefore, if you have any hope of being financially independent and your own boss, you must learn to overcome this cynicism in your life.

1. Forget asking 'what if's'

When it comes to our money, I too often play the 'what if?' game. We ask questions like 'What if things don't go as planned?", "what if I lose control of the money and I can't pay it back?", "What if the economy crashes after I invest this money?" and it goes on and on. Fuelling our "What if?' game is our friends and family who also speak into our life and recommends us that our investments and businesses are too risky, are not a good idea, or will never work. These words of doubt often become so loud that we fail to act; instead, we play it safe.

The 'what if' game is really just noise, yet we allow this noise to distract us from great opportunities in front of us. People in the early 1990s, for example, asked, 'What if we miss out on this hyper dot com bubble craze?', They then spent minor fortunes buying into this short craze without really investigating it's future, why it's all suddenly in huge demand. They became sheep amongst herds that followed the shepherd to be slaughtered financially. Any chance of a stable and strong investment with the dot com bubble never came and that money was lost. If they would invest in financial knowledge first and invested the money in logical investment deals, they would be financially free today.

In order to be rich, you must stop asking 'What if' and start asking 'What is?'

2. Find good advisors

A while ago, a friend James visited me in London at a Property Network, he was impressed with what many successful property investors had done with investing in real estate. He wanted to be financially independent and successful like them. At the time, London real estate was stable yet plenty of discounted deals and mortgages/credit cards were relatively easy to secure. Every lender was trying to get many people to have more credit cards and borrow more easily. He spent a couple of days looking around the city, sourcing for some great opportunities that he calculated and checked if it offers good cash flow, value appreciation, and if it could withstand a recession in his financial situation if it ever came.

James found an investment that he liked, a 2 bedroom flat for £150,000 via a company that specialises in below market value properties, but similar units were going for £185,000 at market value. He found a bargain after he calculated he could afford to make a generous profit with a budgeted refurbishment within 3 weeks, and he called the estate agent to reserve it. He returned to Scotland ready to close the deal on the phone. Two weeks later, the agent still listed the property for sale and confirmed that James had given up on the deal.

I called James to find out what happened. "My family and friends said it was a bad idea and too risky" he told me. "Is your family and friends an investor?" I asked. He replied "No". So, when I asked why James would listen to his non-investors family and friends, he became defensive and simply said he wanted to just watch and wait until he felt 100% ready. Imagine getting rich at that rate!

James' family and friends was a bad choice of advisors, when he allowed their fear to overcome his dream. Often, when we're battling doubt or challenge, our inner cynic will seek out advisors who will fuel and cement our fear with 'What if', rather than with 'What is'. A good advisor such as mentors which can be found via Property networks, seminars and meeting groups, will be knowledgeable and help you see reality.

3.   Focus on the big picture

The successful and financially independent people say "Cynics criticise, and winners analyse."

When I speak to people about investing in real estate, they often tell me they are not interested in real estate, because they don't want to fix the sinks and boilers. Those words are from a criticiser and a cynic.

When someone says 'I don't want to maintain the sinks and boilers." They are saying that little problems like that are more important than their financial freedom, which is the big picture to focus on. I talk about financial freedom and they talk about sinks and boilers. That thinking keeps most people poor.

The rich always find a way or find someone who knows the ways to make their 'I don't wants' into keys for success. For example, I don't want to fix sinks and boilers either, but instead of making that a reason to be trapped in the rat race and financially depend on a job; I find a good property manager that happily fixes sinks and boilers. The rich find ways; the cynic finds excuses. Which one will you be?

4. *Take action*

A cynic says, "I don't want to lose the money", so does nothing. The reality is that they perhaps won't lose money, but they won't make any either. A cynic's inaction keeps him poor.

A while back, a friend in the rat race, told me all the reasons why the price of gold was going up, but he was worried and did nothing with the information, much of which was new to me. He explained that the gold has normally being low in demand before the credit crunch; therefore gold will grow in demand as the economic climate starts to tighten. Later, I returned home, did my own research, verified what he was saying, and instead of worrying, became excited at an early opportunity. With that information, I immediately began looking for and found a reliable gold company that enables me to constantly monitor the gold prices daily. I bought thousands of shares for very little per share and watch it grow exponentially whilst everyone around me started clinging tighter to their jobs and panicking. A few months later into the recession, those shares were growing more than double and the prices per share just kept climbing. When the economic climate begins to show a hint of stabilising, I will be amongst the first to sell slightly before the peak for precaution. While financial knowledge helps you know when it is the right time to buy and to sell, and if it's a logical investment, it's useless if you let your fear and inner rat be your inaction. My cynic friend did nothing but worry. I got good information and acted. The willing gets rich; the panicky stays poor.

5. *Invest in Financial education*

Knowledge is the new money and it's powerful. If your knowledge is trained to see only jobs, then you only have academic knowledge which is risky. You can never own a job, because you can't sell it or buy it. Without rich and financially independent people who own companies, they succeed by buying your time, effort and abilities, and can always have the power to replace you. Which sides do you prefer? It's your responsibility to constantly increase your financial intelligence, because it's your knowledge that makes you rich at the end of the day. This financial knowledge deafens out the noise of fear and doubt. In order to overcome your cynicism, you need to change your thinking; therefore invest in your financial education to help you see in a new way how money works. You must decide which side you are on and then its action time.

STAGE 1: PREPARING THE SMART WAY

Most of us wonder how most investors are wealthy; have the time to enjoy life opportunities and the freedom to do what they want?

The answer is persistence and the right education which is easily accessible for all, because if someone is going on the wrong road, he doesn't need motivation to speed him up. What he needs is the right education to return on to the smart route to financial freedom.

Many people have the impression that most wealthy investors are simply 'fortunate' or they have inherited their money, but truthfully, becoming wealthy or financially free is a plan that you can learn. You will see a glimpse of how the wealthy create, protect and grow their money by using a proven set of systems and principles.

The challenges for most people are the lack of persistence, time constraints and the unrealistic expectations that property investing is supposed to be hassle-free. Therefore, people become discouraged after buying a few standard investment properties and then decide it's more hassle and time consuming than it's worth, or they are wondering why they are working harder than ever, instead of the smarter way to make more money.

Like anything, there are strategies and plans in property investing that works and others that doesn't work. One strategy may progress well for person A, except it's useless for person

B, because of different circumstances and expectations. It's been proven it's possible to earn more money AND more free time, if you learn the right education to become a smarter property investor.

Another vital part of investing successfully to becoming financially free is using leverage, because it allows you to gain more money with less money, more results with less effort, and more time with less time.

If you are currently in the rat race or training to join the rat race, you are an example of leverage to the business owners, because you are being paid a fixed wage to give more of your effort for less time, so the business owners can have more free time. When you know how to use leverage to its ultimate advantage with the right education and persistence, then you understand that it's as equally an important part as having a suitable strategy, for the shortest possible route to financial freedom.

Most property investors starting for the first time, normally begin doing everything themselves, perhaps, some do really well, because they have minimised as much costs, reduced the risks and ensured as much protection. But after learning to be smarter with leverage and still being persistent, they learned that you can achieve more, faster an d with less effort, whist decreasing as much risks as possible. When you think how we only have 24 hours in a day, and a big portion is spent sleeping, entertainments such as TV and bars, commuting, eating and more, you will realise using other people's time, effort and money is more practical.

As you can see, the right education that teaches you how to use and be smart with leverage, and be persistence makes all the differences between the average investor who jumps in without preparations, so he works so hard yet he gets nowhere, and the educated investor who prepares a plan to become smarter, faster, richer for more time. This is the reason why investing yourself with a smart education and being persistence matters so much, because your success depends on it, so, the faster you learn to be financially smarter, the sooner you be repaid in results.

If you want to know which strategy suits you, how to progress better, understand what some of the options are available, then read on. Understandably, the resources for successful property investment plan can vary from person to person, but, I will show you what, how and why the vital parts work. It's certainly not all set in stone and it's different for each individual, but it's the main plan that some of the top property investors I have questioned and studied. Even if you are currently a property investor who already knows almost everything, there is always new knowledge of how to overcome the obstacles and dips.

THE POWER OF LEVERAGE

So the nature of buy-to-let, as with most investments, is being prepared to invest your money for the long term to give your investment the best chance to mature. The Halifax House Price Index seems to verify that previously, property has performed very well over the longer term despite a bumpy duration. Once becoming a buy-to-let investor you need to be comfortable with this risk, because property is not necessarily a one-way bet.

You receive buy-to-let income in the form of a monthly rental payment from your tenants. The rent you can expect to receive from a buy-to-let depends on your property, its location the rental demand and a variety of other factors.

For a buy-to-let investment, income is particularly important as you will have regular costs to cover, so it's extremely important to calculate that your rental income can cover all the cost and still provide you profit. You should also consider putting aside a little each month in a contingency fund. This could cover costs such as redecorating your property in order to attract new tenants and to cover your costs during any untenanted periods.

One-off payments:	Monthly operating costs:
• Stamp duty	• Letting agent's fees
• Valuation/Survey fees	• Mortgage interest(deductible)
• Legal fees	• Landlord's insurance
• Mortgage arrangement fees	• Annual safety checks
• Redecorating fees	• General building maintenance
	• Income tax
	• Capital gains tax
	• Rent insurance (protects you against untenanted periods)

A buy-to-let mortgage allows you to invest in a property with a fairly small amount of money and reap all the gains in house prices rises and income. However, because it's now considered quite normal to borrow to fund a buy-to-let purchase, you need to measure the additional risks that are crucial with borrowing to buy-to-let; risks that may have been overlooked by some investors in the recent house price boom. This risk is exacerbated because the majority of BTL mortgages are on an interest only type and needs to be repaid when the property is sold. So if house prices drop and your property is worth less than the mortgage on it, you would have to pay out the additional cash to repay this portion of the debt by the end of the mortgage term or if you wanted to sell the property.

The advantages and disadvantages of using BTL loan as leverage and gearing (OPM)

If you have a £30K deposit from somewhere and a £100K mortgage as leverage on a £130K buy-to-let property, and that property increases in value by 10% you will have made 43% profit on your original investment of £30K. If the property decreases at 10% loss value, you would lose £45,000 or 43% of your original investment.

If you bought the £130K property without using leverage and the property value increases at 10%—you make a 10% profit on your original investment of £130K, but you *only* lose £15K if that property decreases at 10% in value.

Normally when you invest, the risk you take is limited to the amount you invest—you can't lose any more than you have put in. But as soon as you use leverage, you increase your risk; it now becomes limited to the amount you invest, plus the amount you have borrowed (and any interest due). That means that you could potentially lose far more than you originally invested. You can also receive a rental income while your property appreciates in value. You refinance the asset for tax-free money instead of selling it which could subject your profit to CGT, to purchase more investment properties, so by the second year you could get numerous more investment properties.

Finance sources

There are plenty of choices available when you decide to raise the finance to invest in properties, from no money down deals, seller finance deals to lease option purchases and many more. Having an awareness of the many types of investment deals you didn't know existed could help you make a positive and educated choice that suits you, your circumstances and your investment strategy. A lack of finance, bad credit report or lack of time should not be the reason why you can't invest in properties.

There are many established and creative ways of raising finance, and hopefully you will find some information that can help your own path to financial freedom. There will always be new methods currently forming and in the future. It's important that you define what appeals to you and why, so you can understand what could be the right choices for you. Assess your appeals and the possible choices to achieve them, so you are informed enough to make the right choices if you are offered a better or alternative option.

Most property finance tends to appear so complex and confusing to most people, but it's normally due to a lack of understanding and the unfamiliarity of the methods and jargons. Understanding the methods of how it works, where to find them and understanding what the jargons means, you can begin to recognise how it's possible to find solutions, match it to your requirements and activate it. The main finance normally comes from financial services company in one way or another, although it may need a deposit if it's a mortgage. However funding can be sourced from everywhere and anywhere, if you know the existence of these choices, understand them well and recognise how it could help you.

Some of the many possibilities are:

- Borrow from your friends, family or colleagues.
- Obtain loans or overdrafts
- Credit cards
- Release funds from a pension (usually only works if you are over 50)
- Release equity from your own home or your parent's home
- Obtain a full mortgage or finance from an external provider
- Syndicate the money together with an investment group
- Investment Angels (Similar to Dragon Den method
- Auction finance provider
- Save up your deposit money from your job
- JV partnerships
- Flipping deals
- Bridging loans
- Cash for sourcing property leads and deals
- And more new types forming

It's understandable that finding the seed capital for your first investment is always the hardest, but it's still possible and we all have to start somewhere anyway. When you overcome this challenge, you soon look back at this stage and appreciate that you have done it before, you feel more comfortable about the whole process and more informed and confident about making the right investment decisions. When you have your first investment asset and fund providers will feel more assured about you, because you are more experienced and you can progress in many creative ways. It's worth trying your 100% hardest for your first investment, because the rest will become easier and you will be wealthier when you understand the whole process.

Finances from other people/companies is used as leverage and gearing as it's the best way to maximise your investment potential, because it allows you to have the advantage of the gain on the whole investment when you have merely put in a little of your own cash. Using other people's money (OPM) is how some of the wealthiest Investors such as Donald Trump, Warren Buffett and Robert Kiyosaki have increased their wealth in less time, with less money and with other people effort for the most gain. This OPM opportunity essentially gives you enormous potential than using only your money; therefore the less of your own money you invest in, the higher the return on your money, because you are using other people's money.

Using a couple of hours a week to make more capital reserves:

It is possible to make an unlimited income from selling leads to other property investors, and also if you decide a particular property doesn't fit your investment strategy. Some people have made a career and a business from sourcing leads and property deals for other investors, by advertising heavily to motivated sellers. This works well as a win/win for everyone involved, because if you have the time and effort but want to make more cash, then you can source the leads and deals in the right places. As many property investors who lack the time to source the right properties will pay you between 1% to 4% of the purchase price, depending on the quality of the leads.

The quality of the leads can influence how much money you could earn, because if you pass on just the name, address and property details of a motivated seller that you have not contacted and confirmed their intention of selling, then you would possibly get between £50 and £150 on a specific leads supply website. Whereas, if you have spoken to the seller, assessed the situation, provided a certain amount of background research, preferably you agreed a price in principle with the seller and charge interested investors between 1% to 4% of the purchase price.

Some of the best ways to find those investors, who don't have time to source property deals, is to develop your own network of investors, market through the property investor magazines, and forum websites that specialise in attracting motivated sellers. It helps if you aim for the experienced property investors who know what they are doing and can convert your leads and deals into completed property deals, to ensure that you get paid. You need to be quick in sourcing deals before other investors spot them.

The professional way to request investment money

This is be used and modified with anyone from close friends and family to business contacts, and even people you may know indirectly through friends or contacts.

1. You might be able to help me . . .

2. I am (or we are) starting (or expanding) my property investment business over the next 6 to 18 month . . .

3. I am (or we're) looking to work with a select group of investors/people with funds who can get a better return than they are currently getting from the bank. The rate in the banks in this economic climate is so low, that it's worth considering a better alternative for you and me.

4. The great thing is that the money would be secured in an asset. Who do you know who would be currently interested in making double or maybe more than they currently make on their money?

5. If you do know, could I have their contact details and would you be okay for me to mention that we have spoken and that you suggested I call them? Thanks.

You could add that you are working closely with a Professional Property Mentor who will oversee the projects to completion, because this will give reassurance and confidence to potential investors. You can practice this approach with a friend or family member, to prevent stumbling one of the most important questions you ask for your future. If potential investors refuse to help, just write a list as many direct and indirect people who could help you. Remember, if you don't ask, you don't get!

Make a list of many potential investors as possible and using a few questions prepared before you discuss an opportunity, I would recommend thinking:

- What is your objective of the conversation?
- What leading questions can you ask?
- Ensure that you steer the conversation towards a win/win agreement with both required outcomes.
- Maintain a good relationship, so the person may recommend someone else who can fulfil your requests.
- Arrange a deal that benefits you both securely and reassure any concerns they have by demonstrating on paper, real life examples etc.

TYPES OF MORTGAGES

Mortgages should normally be straightforward, because you simply borrow money to buy a property and then pay the interest on the loan. Though looking at the vast types and criteria requirements to qualify for a mortgage, you perhaps recognise it's a bit confusing. Therefore it's important to understand how each type of mortgages operates, know if it's suitable for your situation and your strategy. In such a hugely competitive market of banks and building societies, they are thousands of lenders waiting for borrowers. To make money and stay in business; they need potential borrowers like you. Change your perspective to accept that they are money out there waiting to find borrowers, than the demand there is from us to borrow that money. All you have to do is ask the right type in the right way, ensure it suits your needs and your strategy. There will be a financial product out there for every type, which suits your specific situation and strategy; it does exist, even if you have to search over a hundred sources for it.

Some of the many types of mortgages that exist are:

- Buy to let (BTL) mortgage
- Fixed rate mortgage
- Interest only mortgage
- Repayment mortgage
- Offset mortgage
- Investment mortgage
- Cash back mortgage
- Commercial mortgage
- Self-employed mortgage

- Self-build mortgage

The preferences for most professional property investors is planning to have enough properties in their portfolio, so paying off a mortgage here or there is possible from either the income they are producing or from capital gain over part or whole of the portfolio. The right mortgage for you will depend on your needs and circumstances, so it's important to understand the options available to you. Normally property investors choose Interest only mortgage, as you can claim back tax on the interest.

Unlike normal domestic residential mortgages that are based on your income even with your partner, the Interest only and Buy to Let (BTL) mortgage is more determined by the property investment. It's usual that the amount you can borrow for a property is 75% LTV (Loan to Value) which means the loan consist of 75% of the property value, although it can vary for your circumstances. The duration of a mortgage can vary for the length of time you prefer such as from 3 or 5 years to decades. If you have a property that has a great return when rented out, a lender will focus more on how it can make a profit for them and for you sufficiently; but for a first-time landlord who is deemed a higher risk, the deposit would be much higher and you may need a higher income for precaution with 3 months of recent payslips, or 2 years account if you are self-employed.

The best ways to qualify for a mortgage can depend on your income sources, certain lenders, the investment strategy you want and how positive your credit report is. As a general rule, the more secure your income, the more choices of mortgage you will have and the lower the interest rate you pay. Although even if you don't have any income, you still have some choices that suit your circumstances and strategy. Therefore if you lack any earned income or you don't want to declare an income or you are self-employed, you may still get certain mortgages; such as a BTL and Self-employed mortgage which is based on the rental income from an investment you want to purchase. It's vital to search for the right financial product for your particular situation.

1. Interest Only Mortgage

You are only paying back the interest on the mortgage, although the loan itself will still need to be paid when the mortgage expires; so it's important to be careful if you are depending purely on the property to increase in value when it can also decrease too. It's expected that extra money is saved into a saving vehicle that is estimated to generate a sufficient return to pay the mortgage when it reaches expiration stage. It's very important to consider and prepare how you repay the capital at the end of the mortgage duration. Most buy-to-let investors have interest-only mortgages, so they're completely relying on equity growth through a generous market, but historical data shows that eventually, property prices always go up. With minimal risk, this type of mortgage is ideal for property investors who can use the straightforward system to help budget carefully and minimise taxes.

Advantages: The monthly payment will be lower, so you have flexibility to use more money elsewhere.

You can purchase a more expensive property with a smaller monthly payment. You can keep your monthly obligations smaller. As a landlord, you pay tax on the rental income (at the normal rate) which you can claim back tax on items including mortgage interest, property management fees and maintenance costs.

Disadvantages: The original mortgage will still be waiting to be paid at the expiration stage; therefore if it can't be paid then the property may be seized by the lender. Interest-only loans may turn out to be bad financial decisions if housing prices decrease, causing you to carry a mortgage larger than the value of the property, which in turn will make it impossible to refinance the house into a fixed-rate mortgage.

2. Repayment Mortgage

This type of mortgage requires higher monthly repayments over an agreed period and when you come to the expiration of the term, you have paid back the entire loan including all the interest on the loan. It's normally over a 25 year term, although it can be varied to your preference; each monthly payment made consist of an interest portion and capital portion. The interest is charged on the capital (principle) amount outstanding and the credit is repaid over the duration of the mortgage. Repayment mortgages are so simple, they would suit almost anybody. If you want the reassurance of gradually clearing your loan each month, then a repayment mortgage is the best option.

Advantages: It's simplicity and clarity is its benefit. At the expiration of the term, you be safe in the knowledge of seeing the money owed reducing, until there will be nothing owed at completion. You are less likely to suffer from negative equity because the mortgage balance will be reducing monthly. You may be able to vary the term of your repayment mortgage. While the standard repayment mortgage term is 25 years you can ask your lender to set yours up to last a longer or a shorter period if you want. Many mortgage providers allow you to make overpayments and lump sum payments, reducing both the interest and capital amounts repayable. This is known as having flexible elements in the mortgage. Most providers offer the option to switch to an interest-only mortgage if you are faced with financial difficulty, such as a loss of income through redundancy or illness. By having repayment mortgages you are able to chip away at the monthly outstanding balance, consequently building your equity. Ensure the rental income covers the mortgage so you don't have to pay out of your own pocket and you will be debt free and will own the property outright when the mortgage comes to an end.

Disadvantages: In the early years your payments are made up of mainly interest so if you decide to repay the mortgage in the earliest stage, then it may look like it hasn't decreased very much. The monthly repayments will be higher than the Interest only mortgage, as it includes both the owed loan and interest. The total repayments typically amount to 2 or 3 times the original capital loan amount, so the total repayments over 25 years on a £200,000 loan would certainly be in excess of £350,000. There may be redemption penalties for making lump sum/overpayments. Long term property investments with repayment mortgages won't be affected by blips in the market. If the market dips and house prices drop, there will still be time to recover. Whereas, short-term investor who has owned a property for 1 year on an interest-only mortgage can easily get into a bracket of negative equity if the market takes a turn for the worst. The investor will either need to hold onto the property or sell at a loss.

3. <u>Buy-to-Let Mortgage</u>

Qualifying for a buy-to-let mortgage depends not on your income unlike conventional deals, but on the estimate rent you expect to achieve with your property investment. Once the rent is more than the mortgage by a certain amount, then you can expect an approval. A BTL mortgage income is usually assessed as a percentage of the mortgage payment, typically at least 125%. So, if your mortgage payment is £500 per month, you need to be getting rent of at least £650, so importantly, the rental value of your property needs to be verified by the surveyor who conducts the mortgage valuation. If you are using a letting agent or property management service to manage your investment, they may on average charge 10% of the rent, or 15% if they are responsible for repairs, complaints and other matters. Landlords could obtain a gross rent equivalent to between 130% and 150% of the rental property's mortgage repayments for precaution Its recommendation are slightly higher, as it requires a profit that landlords need to take into account void periods, maintenance costs, insurance and the daily letting cost.

Sometimes a lender will allow your personal income to be assessed either using what you earn or by assessing your finances to check your 'ability to pay'. A mortgage that is assessed in this way could be the direction to go if you want to have your buy-to-let mortgage on full repayment (as the payment on this is more expensive than the usual method of interest only). Regarding a deposit for the property, the amount you can borrow in relation to the value of the property (loan-to value) is generally lower for buy-to-let mortgages. You may need a significant deposit, likely from 15% to 30% as a down payment, although it can depends on the type of property you want to invest in. The maximum you could borrow is currently 80% of the property's value, compared to a residential mortgage where you could borrow 90%. Ideally you should have up to 3 months worth of mortgage payments, as you need to prepare for any void periods with contingency funds, otherwise you should avoid BTL loans. However, if you are worried about losing money during void periods, many companies may offer insurance which will deliver as much as 6 months mortgage payments if a property remains unoccupied. Even though you may have to budget very tightly without any contingency funds, luckily there are more re-mortgage deals available that can help pay the deposit of a property.

Advantages: The higher you can obtain a rent higher than the mortgage and operating cost, the more likely the approval. Whilst you are earning a rental income, your investment could increase in value and also be used as security to purchase more investments. The duration of the mortgage can vary from 5years to 25 years or more, which offers great flexibility.

Disadvantages: It's important that your outgoings are as minimal as possible otherwise it exceeds the rent. The longer you experience void periods the more it costs you. The property may decrease in value depending on the demands of the market. Lenders may specify that you need a minimum earned monthly income level to give them some comfort that you have other resources to fall on, should you have trouble with under-occupancy or rental arrears. Arrangement fees on buy-to-let mortgages can be a lot higher than on a residential mortgage, with percentage-based fees of up to 3.5% of the mortgage amount charged to secure the cheapest fixed or tracker rates. It's currently very difficult to get a 100% BTL mortgage.

Halifax House Price Index 1992-2012		
Date	Average house price	% change from previous
January 2012	£158,879	-21%
August 2007 (the crest of the wave)	£201,081	+105%
January 2002	£98,088	+50%
January 1992	£65,520	n/a

How do the interest rates vary?

BTL mortgage can comes in a variety of selections such as variables, discounted, capped, tracker, fixed and more. Most mortgages are connected to the base interest rates that are influenced by the Bank of England. The interest rates tend to be announced on news and in the newspaper, and the interests for BTL mortgages may be slightly higher in comparison to normal residential mortgages and it's fairly harder to obtain a 100% BTL mortgage.

- A Fixed Rate mortgage are very popular with first time buyers as they fix rates for the first few years, after which normally the mortgage reverts to a standard variable rate. This enables you to budget accurately and with certainty as the interest rate is fixed for some of the mortgage term. The interest rate is normally fixed for anytime up to 5 years, although if the rates increases above your fixed percentage, then that is great, except when the rates decreases below your fixed percentage.

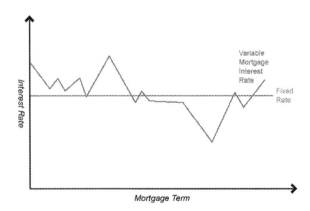

- A Capped mortgage is where the interest rate is capped upwards and downwards (Collared), because the interest rate is capped at a certain maximum level by the lender. A capped rate is normally only for an introductory period—this can be anything from 2-5 years. Once you have finish the introductory capped rate, your mortgage will go onto a lender's standard Variable Rate or a tracker rate for the remaining term, although you can re-mortgage to a new deal if you wish.

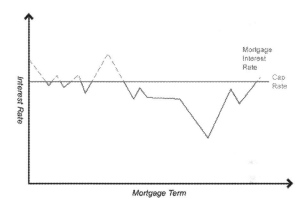

- A Discounted mortgage is where the discount interest rate normally applies for a given period and then reverts to a standard or higher rate, when you get finance at a discount to the base rate or bank variable rate. These mortgages are an incentive if you are a first time buyer who have other initial purchases, so would want to keep payments lower. The lenders are entitled to decrease or increase the rate after the discounted rate ends, so ensure you have budgeted for that stage.

- <u>A Standard Variable mortgage</u> is normally between 0.25 and 1% and it's similar to a tracker as it moves in line with the base rate, but sometimes with a time delay and not always by the same amount as movements in the base rate. Your mortgage lender may also increase or decrease their Standard Variable Rate at any time, so not just after Base Rate changes. Arrangement fees for SVR mortgages tend to be lower than for trackers or fixed rates, so there may be no arrangement fee charged at all.

- <u>A Commercial mortgage </u>could probably be set at a higher interest rate and is generally for larger sums of money than a domestic mortgage, so it generally provided only for commercial properties. It's also more for businesses than for an individual. Lenders generally require a deposit of around 25%-40% of the total value and mortgage terms can run from one year and up to 40 years. Obtaining a commercial mortgage is based on the ability of your business such as a property portfolio business to make the repayments. You will also find that lenders will assess your business before quoting you an interest rate. They generally look at past performance, the current position and long term future plans of the business. The interest rate you will be quoted may be based on these factors and may be higher if the underwriter identifies higher risk in the proposal, so you may need to provide a detailed business plan which demonstrates that you can make repayments, and a professional valuation will usually be required.

- A Flexible mortgage offers flexibility in that you can pay flexible amounts, miss occasional payments, underpay period and overpay when you are able to. The interest rate is generally a standard variable rate, which is charged daily rather than monthly, quarterly or annually so you generally pay less interest. So it provides a lot more flexibility in your mortgage payments, so this works particularly well if you have irregular income. Some variant allows you to draw more money within given limits without having to re-mortgage.

- A Tracker mortgage tracks the base rate specifically, so you may be paying a small amount such as 0.5%, above base and when the base rate rises, so does your mortgage interest and when the base rate is reduced, so does your payments. However the lenders can promptly raise the rates if the Bank of England increases a lot.

- <u>An Offset mortgage</u> can also be called a current mortgage, which is a flexible mortgage where all your financial balances with one provider are added together each day to create a net balance due to the bank. Your main current account or/and your savings account are linked to your mortgage, so generally the lender holds all 3 accounts, but not always. If the balances in your account and/or savings are high, then you pay less on your mortgage, otherwise you pay more on your mortgage. You may be charged interest in this lower balance, so if you have £25,000 on a mortgage and £5,000 on deposit as savings with your lender, you only pay the interest on the net of £25,000. It's a great bonus if you have large amount of cash in your current account, because you are not taxed on deposit interest earned due to not receiving any as the deposit is used to offset against your mortgage loan. If you are a higher rate taxpayer, then this could be a big advantage. A current account mortgage is identical to an offset mortgage, except your mortgage and current account is joined together to appear as a very large overdraft.

- <u>A Cash-back mortgage</u> is more likely for first time buyers as an incentive use the cash back benefit, and it's where the lender offer the cash at the completion stage of purchasing the property. This can vary from a fixed amount example from £200 to £3,000 or a percentage of a loan like 5% of the loan amount. However if you switch from your lender early, then you may have to repay partly or fully of this money.

It would be better if you can manage without this cash back feature, so you can find better deals elsewhere.

Others incentives that some mortgage lenders offer to entice you to borrow with them involves, free conveyance service or a contribution to your legal costs, but they may be a catch as they may require you use their nominated lawyer instead of your own. Another incentive can be a free valuation fee when the lender agrees to lend money, when you allow them to carry out their own valuation on the property. Additional incentive can be free or cheap insurances, although it may be from an alternative lender's business; but be aware if it's only free for a limited time then remove the insurance provider when it expires. Lastly free extras such as certain amount of free furniture, fitting, carpets, bathrooms and kitchen equipment can be provided by the builder as an enticement too. Importantly, check the lender or seller won't add the cost of these benefits to the principle of the loan though. Also you may or may not get some of the benefits, but if you don't ask, then you could miss out.

Choosing the right mortgage for the most returns

Lastly, reflect on some basis calculations regarding mortgage types and amounts, by using a basis illustration you can prove some foundation financial rules for yourself and your strategy, before moving on from the evaluation stage.

Imagine you have a property which is being sold for £67,000. It has a tenant in it paying £500 monthly rent.

Suggestion A—80% Interest only mortgage:

You purchase the property and you agree 80% LTV interest only mortgage of £53,600 at 5%.

Can you calculate your cash on return?

Rent £500

- Minus Mortgage payments £223
- Minus Management fee £50
- Other costs, say £50
  Net monthly cash flow £277

Your annual return is £277 x 12 months = £3,324

Therefore, your return is £3,324, stated as a percentage of your money invested = £13,400 because the deposit is 20%.

£3,324 / £13,400 x 100 = 25%

To begin with, you get much more cash from the property monthly, and the return on your own invested cash is much greater, therefore you instantly see with this simple pattern that interest only mortgages offers two great advantages. But assess this strategy method, because with interest only mortgages you still have to repay the capital amount towards the end.

<u>Suggestion B—85% interest only mortgage:</u>

You purchase the property and you agree a larger mortgage of 85% LTV interest only mortgage of £56,950 at 5%. The deposit would be £10,050.

Can you calculate your cash on return?

Rent £500

- — Minus mortgage payments £237
- — Minus management fee £50
- — Other costs, say £50
- — Net monthly cash flow £163
  Your annual return is £163 x 12 months = £1,956

Therefore, your return is £1,956 stated as a percentage of your money invested, which is smaller at £10,050 because the deposit is 15%

£1.956 / £10,050 x 100 = 19.5%

This suggestion offers you the highest return on your money of all three methods; however you have invested the least.

Understandably, the smaller your cash investment, the bigger the percentage returns, because you are using OPM (other people's money).

Suggestion C—Repayment mortgage:

You purchase the property and you agree an 80% LTV (Loan to value) standard repayment mortgage of £53,600 at 5%. The deposit would be £13,400.

Can you calculate your cash on return?

Rent £500

- Minus mortgage payments £315
- Minus Management fee £50
- Minus Other costs, say £50
- Net monthly cash flow £85

Your annual return is £85 x 12 months = £1,020

Therefore, your return is £1,020, stated as a percentage of your money invested = £13,400 because the deposit is 20%.

£1,020 / £13,400 x 100 = 7.6%

Adopting a property comparable method to financially assess both capital and income strategies:

Constantly do comparable searches before you finally agree to purchase a property and find a minimum five other properties that are comparable to the property you will assess. Ensure they are as close a comparison as possible regarding position, condition, size and location, but also note distinct or peculiar features.

These properties can be found from the internet, agencies, auction catalogues or your own database.

– Property one:
Value (and rental if applicable)   £ . . . . £ . . . .

– Property two:
Value (and rental if applicable)   £ . . . . £ . . . .

– Property three:
Value (and rental if applicable)   £ . . . . £ . . . .

– Property four:
Value (and rental if applicable)   £ . . . . £ . . . .

– Property five:
Value (and rental if applicable)   £ . . . . £ . . . .

Summary averages for the above 5 properties:

£ . . . . £ . . . .

– Compared to the property you are considering buying:
Value (and rental if applicable)   £ . . . . £ . . . .

Does the assessment of the properties compare favourably or not?

Mortgage with refurbishment help

There are many mortgage providers that have renovation or refurbishment style mortgages, so you need to ask around either by calling, speaking face-to-face, online, etc. Even if your usual provider doesn't have this product in their range, then look on the internet or in mortgage magazines for those that does. However, for most home improvements or refurbishment schemes, you likely have to source the money alternatively, but there are some places worth considering obtaining some grants or funding. In all these cases, apply to your local authority or Local Government for information.

- Grants for multiple occupancy housing

This is available for owners and landlords who needs an HMO (House of Multiple Occupancy) grant, which is offered to make houses fit for multiple occupancy. Also a Common Parts Grant is available for refurbishment of the communal areas of HMOs.

- VAT Concessions

There are some VAT concessions, which mainly reduce the VAT applicable to certain refurbishments from 20% to 5% on the costs of refurbishment if the property has been empty for at least 3 years or for properties into HMO, or into residential units. VAT advices are available via HMRC website.

- Community Investment Fund

This organisation supports small local community projects between £10,000 and £100,000 with more details available via www.homesandcommunities.co.uk

- Housing Renovation grants

These are available to owners and landlords with the aim to encourage hosing provision, so the local authority will provide grants to help with certain types of refurbishment, as long as the property is then available for letting for at least 5 years after the receipt of the grant. Your local housing office may provide details for this.

- BARTL (Buy And Refurbish To Let mortgage)

A specific type of mortgage exists for this type of development, so you can find reputable providers offering this.

Releasing equity

It's worthwhile to look at the market to see what else is on offer, because lenders are keen to attract borrowers with a large amount of equity in their homes who can demonstrate a good payment history. Remortgaging is a good way to escape high variable or fixed rates and take advantage of some of the current fixed-rate, tracker or discount mortgages, which have much lower rates. It's also a way to raise funds for investment properties. If you have owned your property for a few years, you could easily unlock a large amount of equity mostly tax free. However remortgaging criteria rules has become tighter since around 2008, so it's a legal necessity to wait six months after the pervious mortgage before remortgaging.

Even if you don't have any available equity or don't own a property, then think about every friend and family member you know who may have some. They probably want to invest in property, but are unsure of how to do it. This is like joint partnering with them to do the time and effort whilst they provide the starting capital for deposits.

Remortgaging could appeal if you are on a variable rate, and believe interest rates are about to rise, then you can move to a fixed-rate deal before this happens. You can visit websites like *www.whatmortgages.co.uk* for a step-by-step guide to Remortgaging.

Remortgaging costs money, and before applying for a new deal, you should find out just how expensive it's going to be. Common expenses are;

- Arrangement and administration fees for the new mortgage, which can vary from £150 up to £2,000
- A mortgage valuation fee, which tends to be between £130 and £300, depending on your chosen lender and the value of your property.
- An early redemption penalty/charge on the existing mortgage. This can be from 3 to 6 months additional interest payments, if you redeem the mortgage within a certain period of time after taking it out.
- Regarding the higher lending charge, if the amount you are borrowing is more than 75% of the property's value (LTV), you may have to pay a one-off higher lending charge (HLC) premium on the new mortgage.
- Solicitor's fees will need to be paid for, unless your new lender offers free legal pack.
- Land registry and local search fees.

If you have negative equity in your property, you will have to find the additional money that you owe on your old mortgage when you take out a new one. If this is the case, don't remortgage unless you really have to. If it's been a while since you last took out a mortgage, you may find that the option available to you now, includes flexible mortgages. These deals give you greater options when it comes to managing your mortgage, such as, giving you payment holidays or underpayments, also, the chance to increase your monthly payments, when you can afford them or make lump sum repayments if times are good. Therefore, you have the opportunity to make additional payments, of saving thousands of pounds in interest and paying off your mortgage early. If you are taking advantage of the opportunity to make underpayments or take payments holidays, you can make the most of fluctuations in your income, or in your payments, to allow your mortgage to fit in with your investment strategy.

Five points plan;

- Write to your existing lender and ask for a written redemption statement, as this will indicate the exact outstanding balance of your loan and shows any penalties/fees to be charged for redeeming your mortgage.
- Calculate what the legal fees involved will be, because these will indicate the exact outstanding balance of your loan and will vary according to the value of the property and the solicitor used.
- Look at the new mortgage offer, including the small print, ask for a written statement of what your new repayments will be. This should show any discounts, all the costs that will be incurred, such as the HLC and any arrangement fees.
- Work out how much you will save each month by taking the repayment for the new loan, but remember that the Standard Variable Rate (SVR) on the new loan will revert to its former form. Take into consideration of how long the discounted tracker or fixed rate continues for.
- To judge if Remortgaging is worthwhile or not, compare the costs with the savings, but don't forget that the costs will be payable upfront, whilst the savings will accrue over a duration of time.

YOUR MORTGAGE PAYMENT COMPARISONS

The table below is an idea on what a 25 year mortgage interest would be like, when calculated annually, which will help you work out your monthly repayments. The interest-only figures don't take into account any other payments into an investment to pay off the mortgage, so you have to customise by adding that part yourself. The longer the term of the mortgage, the lower the repayments will be.

Interest rate %	Repayment mortgage per £1,000	Interest only per £1,000
0.75	£3.67	£0.63
1.00	£3.78	£0.83
1.25	£3.90	£1.04
1.50	£4.02	£1.24
1.75	£4.14	£1.46
2.00	£4.27	£1.67
2.25	£4.39	£1.88
2.50	£4.52	£2.08
2.75	£4.65	£2.29
3.00	£4.79	£2.50
3.25	£4.92	£2.71
3.50	£5.06	£2.29
3.75	£5.19	£3.13
4.00	£5.33	£3.33
4.25	£5.48	£3.54
4.50	£5.62	£3.75
4.75	£5.77	£3.96
5.00	£5.91	£4.17

5.25	£6.06	£4.38
5.50	£6.21	£4.58
5.75	£6.36	£4.79
6.00	£6.52	£5.00
6.25	£6.67	£5.21
6.50	£6.83	£5.42
6.75	£6.99	£5.63
7.00	£7.15	£5.83
7.25	£7.31	£6.03
7.50	£7.48	£6.25
7.75	£7.64	£6.46
8.00	£7.81	£6.67
8.25	£8.97	£6.88
8.50	£8.14	£7.09
8.75	£8.31	£7.29
9.00	£8.48	£7.50

To work out your monthly cost of a £82,000 interest-only mortgage at 6.00%, with a monthly fund input of £75, calculating the following:

82months x £5.00 = £410 plus £75 = monthly total of £485

A repayment mortgage for the same amount at the same rate is worked out in the same way:

82months x £6.52 = £534.64

Your first mortgaged investment

Buying your investment property for the first time can be a daunting experience, because the ability to afford a property has become the biggest problem for those trying to get on the property ladder. Sourcing a deposit is the place to start, since the bigger your deposit, the wider your choice of mortgage loans will be. Also if your deposit is worth at least 5% of the property you want to buy, many more lenders will be prepared to lend to you. However, when a 5% deposit on the average first-time property investors' house is more than £6,000, it can be hard. But some of the many source of finance for borrowing the money for your deposit can be from a bank, building society, or on a credit card. Before your mortgage is agreed, you have to declare the loan with all other monthly expenditure on your mortgage application, which cuts the amount mortgage lenders may let you borrow. In the past, many lenders were happy to lend 100% or even more of the vale of the property, but in today different economic climate, it's extremely rare nowadays, but it will return in the future.

Mortgage lenders have traditionally used income multiples to decide how much to let you borrow, although again, since the housing boom hugely inflated prices, this calculation can produce an affordability 'gap', because house prices have risen beyond these calculations. Now, many lenders that let you borrow based on your 'ability to pay', which sometimes allows applicants to borrow more. Many of these lenders can be found via 'Moneyfacts' website. For example, you have a clean credit record, low expenses and two incomes, obviously some lenders may be willing to lend you more, because you have a higher disposable income.

Incidentally, lenders are often prepared to offer you a little more if you choose a five or ten year fixed rate mortgage, because the monthly repayments stay the same for a long time, which is easier to manage. First-time property investors can be surprised by the entire mortgage-related fees and charges. Mortgage application fees, lender valuations and stamp duty alone can start at anything from £2,000, depending on the property price, and that is before you have even more on to a stamp duty, solicitor fees and surveys. Research has shown fewer than 10% of first time property investors put cash aside for these fees, and so many people pay fees out of their deposit, further limiting their mortgage options. Several lenders offer cash-back or fee-free mortgages for first-time property investors, which provide some welcome cash at a financially tricky time, however rates may be higher on these loans and so may cost more in the long run.

5 points to remember;

- Get some good advice; One of the best ways to help yourself as a first-time property investor is to seek others who are experienced and are mentors who can offer independent and professional advice. Plenty of Property networks and informal meeting groups can be found all over the UK.

- Do some researches in mortgage on the internet by checking out on sites like www.whatmortgage. co.uk and www.moneyfacts.co.uk. Shop around for a mortgage to suit you, your investment strategy and for answers to your questions.

- Find out and arrange funds for the added costs, such as the insurance, furniture, council tax and more.

- Investigate your current financial situation, lists as many options to reduce expenses and improve/add incomes, so you are more likely to manage finances better.

- Never borrow more than you can afford, otherwise it could eat into the resale profit and your funds for the purchase process. So be realistic and strict.

When your lender has confirmed how much you can borrow, add your deposit money to this, to work out your price range. Also you should take into consideration of the purchase costs, such as, valuation fees, survey fee, legal fees, stamp duty, Land Registry fee and removal costs. The cost of buying an investment property soon adds up.

- Solicitor's fees are often round £400

- VAT the lender's valuation fee is likely to cost upwards of £150, depending on your lender

- Homebuyer's report can cost around £450, depending on the size of the property

- Stamp duty cost

- Arrangement fees or booking fees from £60 to £2,000 or more.

All these costs have to be accounted for when deciding how much you can afford to pay for a property, but ensure you obtain a quotation in advance of instructing a solicitor or surveyor to carry out work for you.

Stamp duty;

One of the biggest costs associated with purchasing a property is stamp duty, as this is paid to your solicitor who passes it on to the Stamp Office; however at the time of writing, there is no stamp duty to pay on property purchase below £125,000. The duty is 1% of the price of properties costing between £125,001 and £250,000, 3% for those up to £300,000, 4% for properties costing between £500,001 and £1million, and 7% for properties over £2million. However, properties over £2million purchased by certain persons, including corporate bodies, have to pay 15% in stamp duty. Although, there are some areas where property purchases up to the value of £150,000, don't attract stamp duty, but your solicitor should be able to tell you if the chosen property is exempt.

Higher Lending Charge (HLC);

When a mortgage exceeds a certain percentage of the valuation of the property, usually 90%, although it could be higher, you may be required to pay a one-off fee. This is the HLC which covers the lender, if you default on your mortgage. The fees varies from lender to lender, but can be substantial, but the fee is normally paid on completion, although, it could be added to your mortgage.

Insurance;

Another outlay to consider when buying an investment property is the cost of insurance, such as the types available are;

- Buildings and contents insurance; your lender will insist the property is covered by buildings insurance and you will be asked to provide evidence if this is the case. Contents cover is optional, but if you buy household insurance, you will get both types of cover.

- Life insurance; this can be set up to pay off your mortgage in the event of your death. If the policy is set up purely to cover your mortgage, you can cut your monthly premium by opting for term insurance, rather than whole-of-life policy.

- Mortgage payment protection insurance (MPPI); this will cover your mortgage repayments, if you have an accident or are sick and unable to work, or you are made redundant. This cover usually lasts for up to 12 months.

Is it possible to have more than one mortgage per property?

It's possible to have more than one mortgage per property and they don't need to be with the same lender, providing the terms and conditions of each mortgage allows for multiple mortgages. There is no legal limit to the number of mortgages you wish to have. You recognise that the first or original lender will have 'first charge' over the property and the subsequent mortgages will have second charges. Generally you can see all the charges that are attached to your property via the land registry website by the UK Government. You can have several mortgages on each property, and you have several charges over the property registered. Therefore if you have a mortgage with a bank, added with a loan from a family member to pay for the deposit, then they would both be valid charges on the register. However check with each lender if they agree with this, as not all of them do.

It's important to understand the priority of charges over a property and they specify the order in which the money is distributed, just in case the property gets repossessed so the mortgage is defaulted. Therefore the first charge lender gets the first seize of the money, subsequently the second, and then a third lender if they are involved, until what's left over for you. Be aware that when you clear a mortgage that is paid off, check that the lender removed the charge at the Land registry, which sometimes forgotten to be updated.

Be aware that if you want multiple mortgages, perhaps a line of credit or block of mortgages may be better suited for you and your strategy. Example you could get a mortgage lender who arranges a 'pre approved' block of 10 mortgages or a block of mortgages worth £200,000, to be used and drawn down as and when you find the right properties. However the lender will still want to conduct their survey on each property as it appears, but you have to process the application procedure each time. Furthermore, this method of block approach could show a cleaner position on your personal credit file, as it shows one transaction instead of several.

What can I use as security for a mortgage?

Basically anything that the lender will define as a security and it can be from overseas such as your holiday home.

- The property you are purchasing
- Your existing property portfolio (if you already have one)
- Other assets or businesses that the lender will accept as security
- Other income streams in the form of a guarantee
- Your existing home (perhaps s a second mortgage)

Who can qualify for a mortgage?

Almost anybody can qualify for a mortgage, because there is an abundant choice for so many types of circumstances. Example great or bad credit report, low or irregular income, any age above 18 years old, for building properties, ecologically friendly projects and accelerated mortgages that offers stage payments as you develop or renovate the property. Also if you are buying at an auction, listed properties, incomplete, new build and even for conversion. You can type in a specific mortgage type via Google and a huge variety of lenders fitting your requirement to be checked out, with new ones appearing weekly. There will be one of the various thousands of financial mortgages that exist out there that will fit your specific situation and strategy.

It's important to be aware of the additional costs of obtaining any type of mortgage, but each will vary in prices and if you know what to expect, then you can be more financially prepared.

- <u>Insurances</u>

  Occasionally lenders will try to guide you towards their own insurance arm, example for the buildings insurance, or accident, sickness and unemployment insurances. But be aware that lenders cannot insist it as a condition of any loan that you take their particular insurance or other service; otherwise it's a breach of the relevant legislation. However they can make the loan conditional upon you taking out some appropriate buildings insurance.

- <u>Lenders' valuation fees</u>

  Normally the lender will always insist on getting their own valuation for any property that they lend on, however they need this valuation for their own purposes, but you generally have to pay for it. If the deal falls through, then this fee is not refundable.

- <u>Booking/arrangement fees</u>

  This is normally paid to the lender and is attached to the loan application form. It may be a fixed amount or a percentage of the loan amount requested, but the booking fee isn't refundable if the loan is not granted. Arrangement fee tends to be the fee charged by the lender at the other end such as when the loan is granted to you and these fees are commonly seen on fixed or capped rate mortgages.

- <u>Early redemption charge or penalty</u>

  Usually when a discounted or capped interest rate is offered, you find that there is an early redemption charge/penalty also attached to the loan. So for example, there may be a penalty for redeeming the mortgage early that can be significant, like 6 months interest, or refund of the total benefit or discount received. Clearly redemption penalties are aimed to lock in the customer for as long as possible. A redemption 'overhang' is where the penalty clause is for a longer period than the original benefit. Therefore a redemption penalty is in force for example 4 years, when the discount rate is applied for 2 years.

- <u>Mortgage indemnity charge/guarantee</u>

  This is known as the high percentage fee, where some lenders insist on you paying this fee or charge if they feel that the amount borrowed is too close to the actual value of the property. Example, you get a 95% mortgage, the lender may ask for you to pay for this guarantee that if the value of the property decreases, then the lenders' money is protected by the guarantee. Therefore if the time when this guarantee is requested occurs, the lenders directly get the money.

- <u>Other fees and charges</u>

  There is plenty more as the fees and charges vary from lender to lender, and it will be called many different things; so it's important to be aware before signing anything and ask questions about them for clear explanations.

Bridging Finance

When some property investors talk about acquiring properties without or little of their own money down before the beginning of a different economic market, or getting all your cash out when completing a deal, you will often hear that this is no longer possible or allowed by the lenders following the credit crunch. It's not a case that you can't use these strategies anymore, you just have to explore the new and adapted ways, which are also practical and acceptable in the current market. Most property investors are used to acquiring a property with the intention of getting their deposit money back out with and tax free profit released via refinancing, before moving on to buy the next property immediately. They could repeat this process at speed allowing them to accumulate a portfolio without or little of their own money tied up in each deal. This strategy can be used to buy to sell or holding exit plan. Selling the property and paying off the bridging loan whilst keeping the difference as profit or letting the property. The property will generate rental income but there are no monthly payments to make, because these will have been deducted from the gross advance of the bridging loan at completion.

<u>Bridging loan with refurbishment</u>

Bridging loan is useful if you don't want to be forced to wait 6 months before you can remortgage against the higher end value if it has increased in value due a refurbishment. Having your capital and refurbishment costs tied up whilst the property is rented out in the meantime may sound acceptable, but you will have to convince the lender that the value of the property has increased with supporting evidence, before being allowed to refinance it. Due to this particular way of finance structure, it works best on deals that offers the potential to add serious value.

It's not as complex as it sounds when I break down the process in stages, so imagine:

1. A purchase price is agreed with the vendor.

2. Bridging finance is agreed in principle after the lender has been shown the deal and the usual cost is around 1.5% monthly for the agreed time. At this point, bridging loan will be agreed against the full market sale price, whereas a BTL mortgage would only lend against the purchase price agreed with a vendor.

3. Contracts are exchanged but with a delayed completion. Remember, a deposit is normally required to exchange which is about 10% or less as standard, which is the investor's cash.

4. There is a clause in the contract which allows works to be carried out on the property between exchange and completion.

5. The investors carries out the works, the cost of the works is also funded by the investor.

6. The property is surveyed but valued on its post refurbished value, not on the purchase price. The investor would be able to take out a loan to acquire

the property and cover the refurbishment costs at the completion point, therefore refurbishment are not left in the deal as they would be, had the purchase been funded with a BTL mortgage.

7. The investor completes on the property taking out the bridging finance, but remembers at this point, that some or all of the deposit and refurbishment cash is returned to the investor.

8. The property is sold on the open market at its full value or if you want to let it first, then it can be refinanced with a traditional BTL mortgage after 6 months. There are no monthly payments to make whilst generate rental income, because these will have been deducted from the gross advance of the bridging loan at completion.

9. If you let your property out for a minimum 12 months which will qualify you as an experienced landlord according to commercial lenders, then you don't need to wait 6 months, therefore this could significantly lower the cost of a bridging finance.

Bridging loan without refurbishment

If you have purchased a property in good condition, doesn't require improvement, but are off market and you purchased it with a deep discount of around 40% from the true market value. Therefore, this strategy works best if you intend to buy to sell without any or little refurbishment work, which is exactly like a flipping method.

The benefits of this strategy are:

- If you want to complete in a matter of days, it's essential to work with a solicitor who has experience in bridging.

- The bridging lender will lend against the open market value rather than against the purchase price.

- It helps if the property is not on the market, because the lender will send a surveyor out, therefore if the surveyor sees the property on the market for £10,000 more than you are paying for it, because if you tell them you are paying £40,000 less than its worth, then you risk undoing the deal.

- Loan to value could be 65% of the open market value minus the costs (setup fee and monthly payments for the agreed terms), because these costs are deducted from the gross advance.

- The rates of bridging loans are generally in line and comparable to most bridging products, despite monthly costs being higher than the high street BTL lenders, the requirement on cash is significantly reduced. Arrangement fees tend to be 2% and a broker's fee would be 1%.

Basically, you find a property off market worth £100,000 and the bridging lender will advance 65% of the value less costs (net advance circa £59,800). Whereas, if you have agreed a purchase price of £65,000 in a standard purchase, you would be expected to put in £16,250 which is 25% deposit plus legal costs, arrangement fee and survey costs. Therefore, your total cash input in this as standard purchase would be around £18,000. Whereas, you would only have to put down around £7,000 including legal fees if you are using the bridging strategy.

AUCTIONS

Most properties featuring at auctions are generally repossessed, cosmetically undeveloped, structurally undeveloped and even completely developed and rented with a mixture of commercials, lands, residential properties as freehold and leaseholds at various prices. It's important to understand why the seller wants to sell a property, because it's likely not a profitable enough investment for them anymore. Perhaps, if it's making a rental income, will it meet your minimum return targets? Furthermore, the motives for selling any properties could be any reasons, such as job relocation, redundancy, divorces or business changes, and more. Therefore, it's vital to know what the reasons are to understand if it will affect you and your investment portfolio in a good way or a bad way. An example of an opportunity is a property that requires cosmetic improvement, has development potential, situated in an up and coming area with a motivated seller you could negotiate with, and you have calculated it could be profitable. Even if you don't see many of the types of properties at the auction or people constantly outbid you for them, there are always more available than only at the auctions. Remember you make your money when you buy, not when you sell.

It's very important to know when to stop bidding, otherwise you erode too much of the profit potential, because you certainly don't want a property that ultimately costs you. It's not always about the location, but how good a deal is by knowing when to stop bidding by setting a minimum target and you could find many undervalued properties. You can make an offer on a property before, during and after the auction.

Remember these crucial steps before you rush into anything:

–   Familiarise yourself with auctions and understand how it functions, whilst recognising who are the professional lenders and investors are, and you can discuss some deals with the finance lenders there.

–   Obtain the catalogues from at least 3 different auctions in advance, which are usually free, match the properties and locations to your requirements and prepare some questions to help you decide if it's the right investment for your strategy.

–   Decide which properties you view and go view them with your prepared questions.

–   Obtain the legal pack, because an awareness of the formal terms and conditions vary for each auctions.

–   Consider your minimum targets and maximum bidding limit by looking at the guide price and decide where you plan to stop bidding.

–   Deposit is a minimum of 10% or £1,000

–   Calculate and arrange your finance, after you now know how much you require.

–   Take personal identification, money, and register to bid

–   Completion of purchasing a property takes 28 days maximum.

- It will be your responsibility to necessarily insure the property.

- Get the property surveyed.

- During and after the event, ensure you record and analyse the guide prices, reserve prices, withdrawn prices, selling prices, because you can understand how property investors invest and learn useful points for next time.

If you can source enough potential properties then you have volume on your side, so imagine, you want to purchase a property at £40,000 intending to spend £5,000 and then sell it. You know that when refurbished, it should be at least £50,000 after the time it needs to refurbish. If you can source only one potential property that matches your criteria and it's for sale at £59,000 you can offer the seller £40,000 but if they refuse, then you don't have a property. However, if you can source 10 of these potential properties with the same minimum percentage of returns, all for sale between £45,000 and £52,000 then you only need one seller to accept and you have your property. When you can source and offer on 10, you increasingly acquire more for your particular strategy. Overall, the more numbers of potential properties you find, then the more it gives you buying strength.

Whilst you refurbish the properties, remember that for every month you hold these properties, you are eating into your profits as you are likely to be paying lending interests on the finance, so speed is essential here. Treat the properties like hot potatoes; you need to move them quickly before it gets cold. Spend only as minimal as possible on the purchase price and refurbishing price, to obtain the profit that you need, either to increase the potential rent or capital gains.

You are generally required to place 10% deposit when your bid is accepted, and provide the remaining of the money within 28 days. It's possible to obtain funds from auction lenders who can process the application within 28 days, although it's advisable to discuss the property you want with the lender at the earliest stage before the auction day. There are many properties and lands that are approximately priced from very little and onwards, so it's worth checking out if you want to start small. However, it's not always about the price, but how well it can be a return on your investment. Auction lenders can be found advertised in auction magazines, brochures and online

JOINT VENTURE PARTNERSHIPS

Partnering with a JV partnership can widen your possibilities, because it allows you to think bigger than what you could do alone, such as access to variety of investment opportunities, more quantities, better networks of suppliers and contracts, more time to find great deals, more money to fund projects. A joint venture makes the most of leverage; therefore there is no limit to what you can achieve with the right joint venture. When you prove your reputation of being reliable and great at what you do, people will soon bring deals to you.

Before you decide to explore and arrange with a potential JV partner, you need to know what you have to offer, what you require and what is really important. Then you search through some networks of property investors to identify your potential partners, which is someone who has what you need and needs what you have. Finally, you ask what is important to that person when you identify the potential partner, consider the type of deals you both want to do and then agree on a win/win arrangement.

Joint venture are normally for people who are either cash poor and time rich or cash rich and time poor. You don't have to do everything alone, because there are people who value their time and people with a rich mind-set will spend their money to save time. This is practical if you want to focus on the things you enjoy and you excel at, but prefer to delegate the other tasks to someone who can do it better and quicker for you. All partners in a JV partnerships must bring something different, be open and honest in the relationship. Therefore ensure you both have thorough documents that outline how the partnerships will work and who is responsible for specific tasks. Ensure you detail the inputs from each partner, the timescales and deadline involved. Clarify the financial arrangements, cash flow requirements of the project, the expected returns, that the potential risks can be limited and what will the profit share be. Not only is the duration of the partnerships is important, also a clear exit strategy needs to be agreed on to know how and when the partnerships is completed. Ensure you prepare a contingency plan if things don't go to plan. Ensure this is all written as an agreement to avoid a danger of any confusion in the future due to a verbal agreement. Understandably, it is important to build an honest and open relationship if both of you are hoping to complete a project as smoothly as possible.

VARIETY OF STRATEGIES

DETERMINATION ATTRACTS SUCCESS

We can all find books containing the habits of what and how successful people manage, and overcome the difficulties in the journey of reaching their goals. Your success and dream is very important to you, so it helps to practice the habits of successful property investors to improve your productivity and make yours and your loved ones lives better as a result.

- Your purpose to live your dream:

    Understand why you have that reason to work on your dreams, whilst others dream with their eyes closed, and why you are sacrificing a safe life for a risky one without ceilings and limits to success. If you don't know, just ask yourself why by looking at your core, emotional reason for creating a better change for the future. Many of the greatest accomplishments in the world were created by ordinary and nervous people like you, but the desire was stronger than the fear, that failure was unthinkable.

    Imagine if Abraham Lincoln hadn't believe he was capable of living his dream to give America it's freedom and a better future, just because he accepts he's a poor and illiterate person. Thanks to his strong desire to overcome this pointless fear, he is known as one of history's great men for following his dream for himself and others.

- Against all odds:

  The one thing that defines the truly successful from the 99% of the population, who never reach their true potential, is an unbreakable faith and what they are doing is right. Even the best of us question if our dream is going to come true and when it will, so we all have our moments of doubts. The important part is to drown your doubts and fears, while others keep listening to it, until it breaks them down and just quit. So have your moments of doubts, because you are only human, but just don't let it control and decay you. Instead, use it as a motivation to prove the winner in you is stronger.

- Keep going whilst others quit:

  What separates plenty of the great people we read about in history books, even from those we've never heard of and those who really struggled still kept going. They only stopped when they reached their dream, and even then, they may create a new mission, so quitting was never an option. How does the person who gave up on his dream, know how long it would have taken him to become a success? It could be tomorrow or 10 years. He doesn't and never will know. None of us do.

  Imagine Nelson Mandela, who didn't achieve his greatness or success early on in his career or in life like some. Like others, he achieved it after surviving while others died or quit, and it wasn't just about what he does best, but also the best for what he endured. So, even if he struggled and felt hopeless in the meantime, he was still the last one standing. We don't know when our breakthrough will come, so don't confirm your failing by quitting. You can change, evolve or adapt, but don't ever give up on your dream.

- You do it for you and your loved ones:

  The truly successful in life always get there, because they created a better change in the lives of others, not just their own. 'Objects' can be a motivator or rewards, but they can't be just the only motivation, because if something worthwhile drives you greater than just the things you can finally afford, then you try harder, longer and give more input. Purely just making money is very materialistic and only improves your life and others physically, but if you are trying to make more time to be with loved ones, enjoy the journey of achieving your dream, not be financially trapped and dependent on a job, and so on, then that is better don't you think?

- Have the energy to thrive;

  Generally, the more energy you have, the easier it is to focus and the higher the quality of your work is. Keeping physically fit gives you greater blood flow to your brain, enhancing alertness and improving focus. Make training a part of your life, even if it's a small effort and time portion, as every little helps to fuel your energy, thus more effort input on the process.

- Learn from the best:

Every successful person from Usain Bolt to Warren Buffett and so many others studied their abilities as much as possible, Warren Buffett invested hours upon hours studying other successful people his whole life, who have excel in the same category. It's not about what the limits are, but what they can do if they learn how. Study the habits of the people who inspire you, and put in the work to be the best of what you can do with the habits. When people think of Usain Bolt, they think of a human bullet for being the fastest athlete in the world, but we fail to see the student first. Very few invested so much time and effort like him in running. Both were a student first, a success second. We were all born with a brain but how well and how long you train your mind to think like a success makes all the difference.

If you are trying to sharpen your abilities and be your best in property investment, then study the best people who have prepared and succeeded in that category. Otherwise, being a drone that simply goes through the motions is no way to achieve greatness. If success is something you want as bad as you want to breathe, then learn whatever it is from inside and out, build a wealth of knowledge and eventually the result will be a great and inspiring work.

- No risk, no reward:

  It's true that those who have achieved real success have often risked the most to get there, yet billions of us have the talents or abilities to achieve greatness, but were missing the gut to risk going for it. It could be just getting house of your dreams, so you decide to leave your career to make more money in a business. Or it could be more ambitious, such as trying to provide free healthcare and education for millions in a developing county. Whatever your dream is, give it enough of an effort to be realised, because if you don't take a chance, then you won't stand a chance.

- Excuses are harmful:

  We're the victim of injustice from time to time in life, such as it could being denied the promotion that we deserve, and too many others to mention, but no matter who you are, we all get treated unfairly in life at some point. You choose one of either choice; you either feel sorry for yourself, or you push forward anyway and learn from it as lessons to motivate you. We all have two voices, where one voice tells you to keep going even in the face of immense challenge, to focus on the dream step by step and believe in yourself. However, we also have the voice that tells us to do unhelpful things too often, like what's on television, or go shopping, or unwind too much.

  Imagine if Nelson Mandela used his unjust imprisonment as an excuse to give into his anger, but constructively he used it as an opportunity to learn, grow, and eventually free others. So understand why you have your excuses and how you can use them in a constructive way.

- Values:

   Identify what values you have that guide your life through tough times, and when things couldn't get any better, because those are the values that should always remain, at your core, and you shouldn't change who you are. Winston Churchill had values, but the difference between him and everyone else, is that he kept to his values at all costs. He didn't change who he is and his values when they weren't popular, which is a rarity in this world. You should know what your values are and live by them.

- Early mornings and late nights:

   Your determination to accomplish your dream is first and foremast, so until it's complete, everything else comes second. There is no substitute or short cuts to success, so you have to work for it or hire people to help you achieve it.

Stage 2: Action and diversify

On the growth forecast chart, the curves indicates the planned speed and progress, whilst the lines indicates the actual speed and progress, and what you can do when you under-perform or exceed the goals along the way. Therefore, with the right education to invest smarter with leverage and remain persistent, then you will eventually see advancing results, but don't wait for results before you can start to believe, or you will be waiting forever. Prepare and believe now and the results will show.

Each individual stage will have dips and peaks, because even the best laid plans never go perfectly, so all you can do is prepare for the best and worst times. If you don't overcome the worst times, then you get stuck and slowly decay, but when you get the peaks, you can protect and reinvest into a bigger snowball effect. Of course, everyone will experience the dips and the peaks at different stages and at different speeds, because some will result in almost £30 million created within 10 years, and some will create £4 million in 15 years, therefore it's depends on you to control and boost this process.

If you are expecting instant results after all the preparations for the property investment plan, you need to give it time to mature like a fine wine. Meanwhile, be patient and within 12 months, you see the parts forming into a result. It doesn't happen overnight and you don't want to cut corners where it matters.

This is when most people give up, because the results wasn't instant and excuses such as lack of money or time shouldn't stop you. There are always new solutions and alternatives to every problem. Remember to keep updated with the fast moving times while you control and boost your property investments, or you get left behind like yesterday newspapers, which explain why top property investors continuously learn smarter education and adapt for the future.

Focus like a laser on your goal with the help of a strategy and excel at it, otherwise what happens if you juggle all four different strategies at once? You spread yourself too thinly and it's overwhelming.

Understandably, you could feel discouraged when you have spent so much on legal fees, down valuations, getting them tenanted, void periods and deposits when you have purchased your first few properties, that you wonder if it's worth all this hassle and where is the instant returns? Even smart property investors experience this at the early start, but minimising obstacles is all a natural part of making progress, but you are on the right route to eventually see results.

I am sure you have got many questions such as, 'Isn't it wise to have a plan B strategy if the main strategy fails me?', 'I need to make instant income now, so I need instant results now!' or, 'How many strategies is too few or too many?' and so much more.

The answer is to delegate by adopting the 70/20/10 principle, but I recommend it as a guide only, it's 70% of your working time on the main strategy, 20% on your secondary strategy, and 10% on updating your knowledge of changing times and smarter methods that can benefit you. If you focus only 40% on the main strategy, then you risk slowing the progress, but if you focus 100% on it, then you become too dependent and attached to it. Therefore, you want to diversify with perhaps 10 or more BTL HMOs properties giving you a boosted income, then set up a management system around it, so you can park it and forget it, and then focus 70% on the secondary strategy. Remember you can't move onto the next strategy until you have systemised your first strategy. After the main strategy has met its minimum target of creating steady and passive incomes, then it's time to focus on the next one. The secondary strategy will be achieved much quicker and easier until it fulfils its target, because you have already experienced how to do it for the main strategy. Adopting this principle from the beginning can gives you a head start, because once you know how to do it after the first time, it will be quicker and easier for the following strategies, due to the law of compounding.

Sooner or later, you could start to see some peak times of income rolling in from the rents, or turnover in your portfolio building business. Some of you may decide to stop and keep it static, which is fine, but what works now may not work in the changing future. Instead, you may prefer to master and fine tune the secondary strategy to keep you ahead of the competition and benefit from the changing market.

Boosting your portfolio growth

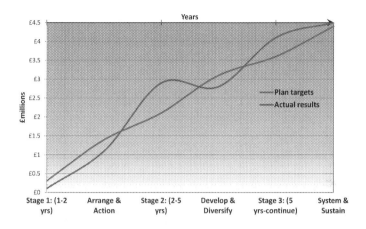

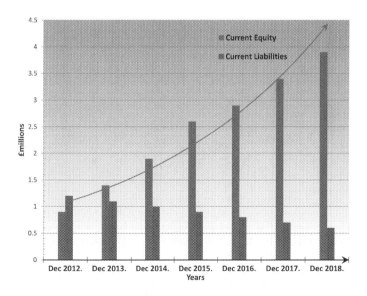

	Year growth of %	End of year 2012	Dec 2013	Dec 2014	Dec 2015	Dec 2016	Dec 2017	Dec 2018
Current Equity								
Current Liabilities								
Balance								

CHOOSING A STRATEGY THAT SUITS YOU

It's important to think very clearly about your entire strategy for purchasing properties at this step, because there are numerous ways to financially evaluate the property deals you are considering. The variety of strategy that you adopt will define the evaluation method you decide on. If your strategy is a capital version, then the yield figure will be entirely irrelevant. Likewise, if you have an income generating strategy, obviously you will need a yield type evaluation method. Keep your evaluation as simple as possible; providing you use your method constantly for ease, then you will need to start with the end in mind.

You could accumulate rental properties in the background to act as a pension for your retirement income, whilst having the choice to continue in paid employment. It's very important that you get high income producing assets; therefore, to evaluate each property on its income potential is vital, if you prefer the option to discontinue your job and depend on the property income. You might want a mixture of income and capital growth, in which case a mixture of evaluation methods may work.

You will need to consider what you are planning for the property once you acquire it, so decide what the investment strategy for each property is beforehand. One or some of the many strategies you will like to consider could be:

- Buy to refurbish to sell (capital)
- Buy to sell (capital)
- Buy to let (income)
- Buy to build to let (capital and income)
- Buy to refurbish to let (capital and income)

Understandably, for every single type of exit strategies you will need to consider a different financial evaluation, because any property that needs refurbishment requires you to acknowledge costs, materials and labours. To acquire an opportunity that provides an immediate income with no additional outlay; is by purchasing already tenanted properties.

To match a financial evaluation tool that fits your investment strategy; question yourself why you are doing this and you will know what your preferences are. You will need more than one financial evaluation tool, if you have more than one strategy performing.

Certain evaluation tools are very problematic and some are very easy. It's imperative to find the method that works for you, because there are various different methods of evaluating property investments for different properties. It's more important to find one that you are at ease with and that you can apply often and fluently, rather than evaluating properties with complex systems that are problematic to complete.

The Importance of a smart exit strategy

The key difference between the average investor and the smart investor is numerous things; but mostly its education and planning. To be a successful lasting property investor, you treat the activity as a business and not as a hobby or half-heartedly. Importantly, you will need to take not just your business, but also yourself seriously too.

To define the long-term investment strategy you need to start with the end in mind. To discover what the end is for you, ask yourself and answer these questions such as:

1. What portfolio value you are aiming at?
2. When do you intend to stop? If ever?
3. How will you know when the project is finished?
4. Will you ever retire?
5. Why do you want to do this?
6. What do you want this business to be at the final stage?
7. How much do you actually need for basis each month to live?
8. How many properties do you want?
9. Have you considered the tax implications of an exit strategy, such as IT, GCT and IHT?

Answering these questions will deliver the strategic targets to aim, and then start identifying the steps of how to achieve those targets which will deliver the specific action steps to take.

Many will say that you can't really form or manage any property investment business successfully without having a strategic plan in action; therefore the indicator of the smart outlook is the awareness of strategic and business planning.

The strategy is necessary for you as an investor and it also has other purposes: it can act as a constant reminder to save you on track and it can also form the foundation of a business plan, which can be used for other purposes such as financing. Unquestionably, you will know that to accomplish the completion of any goal or objective, you will at least need to identify what that goal is. Forming your property investment strategy defines those goals and objectives visibly and upfront.

Your key option is having either numerous smaller and regular amounts of money (income) or to have bigger but possibly irregular amounts of money (capital). Therefore, you consider the two fundamental strategies of income and capital, and some methods of how to combine them. You will intend to generate cash surpluses monthly with income, so that you don't need to completely depend on your job. With capital strategies you are looking for more than income, so what you will prefer is a lump sum of capital at the end.

Discovering the particular strategy for you can be a challenging process, and could also change with your personal life. Investing in property is a massive field and there are numerous different investment strategies to choose from, and there are constantly new strategies being developed. However, regular good training can reveal you to many different strategies from which you can select the most suitable for you.

The fifth question is the most important one as normally it gives you the enthusiasm for what you do. Although, superficially, you will say that you invest for money, very rarely is this the only reason. Most people have a larger, more essential goal which involves some measure of personal freedom, so remember to maintain the larger goal in mind to overcome the obstacles during the journey to success.

It's extremely important to consider what your exit strategy will be; because you could be paying more tax than you have to if there is an alternative, more tax-efficient strategy. As an example of many possibilities, instead of selling the properties which could subject you to CGT, you could remortgage against it, because this debt is tax-free, whilst receiving its rental income.

Creating urgency and action

If there is one thing that grips people back on their journey to create life changes and form financial independence, it's lack of urgency. You have the ability to create financial security and financial independence within a few years if you are focused, plug into a proven system, have a professional mentor discuss with you to assess your strategies to maintain your urgency.

A ten-year goal doesn't create enough urgency for you to take action today; your goals needs to be within 12 months or 24 months.

Commanding questions to help you form urgency:

- How will life be in 12 months? If you choose the choice to stop working, to go part-time or to step away from your business, will you now have more time freedom?
- How BADLY do you want that?
- What has to change NOW in your life?
- What are you frustrated with that you really want to change and that your property business will help you overcome?
- If you build your property business, will your situation change or will it remain exactly the same?

Define and complete the income part of your strategy first, followed by the capital part, ensuring that there is enough income to support you whilst you grow the business. Most people then relax after there is enough income, as the pressure to survive decreases and therefore, you make much better and stronger investment decisions across your whole property portfolio.

Another crucial key to getting a good financial deal is in the sourcing, therefore if you can source 100 properties of the similar type for your portfolio, you have strength when negotiating the purchase price, as they will always be somebody out of 100 sellers who will accept a low price, which matches your strategy. If you only source one property, then the seller has all the negotiating strength.

Set yourself a minimum income amount per property monthly, and refuse any properties that fall below this, when looking at rental properties. Set your guide lines in terms of returns of cash inflows, percentage returns and capital requirements and strictly stick to them. It makes the investing simple and emotionless if you have a method or system of returns and calculation that you stick to.

Ensure a balance within your portfolio and strategy, because you certainly need money now and in the future for retirement, sending children to school, etc. You never know how your life will change in the future, so you need some financial guarantee for the unpredictable times, therefore form a contingency and balance your strategy from the start. Balance income and capital, organised with short-terms and long-term investments, because this will protect you as much as possible from most outcomes.

Begin with small deals and build up to bigger deals, because there is essentially nothing wrong with big deals, and obviously, bigger deals can offer you bigger profits in the end. Though, when you are still learning in the early stages, it's safer to learn on small deals rather than big ones. Smaller deals won't completely destroy you, but a large deal could bankrupt you if you get it wrong. Just like it's advisable to walk before you can run, begin with small low risk deals and move up to bigger risk deals when you are comfortable and ready.

For every person who wishes to invest, there is a different strategy for everyone. No two people are 100% identical, so no two strategies will ever be 100% identical, but I guarantee that the more you practice, the smarter your investing will be.

YOUR FINANCIAL ROADMAP

Income	Current	Goal (the minimum and when?)
Earned Income		
First		
Second		
Earned total		
Portfolio Income		
Royalties		
Interest		
Dividends		
Portfolio Total		
Passive Income		
Business (net)		
Real Estate (net)		
Total Income		
Expenses (optional)	**Current**	**Goal**
Car loan/purchase	£	£
Holidays	£	£
Utilities	£	£
Maintenance	£	£
Insurances	£	£
Clothing, Social & Indulges	£	£
High bills & foods	£	£
Gadgets, items of value	£	£
Credit cards for treats	£	£
Car running costs	£	£

Personal loans	£	£
Other	£	£
Total expenses	£	£
Net monthly cash flow Total income—total expenses		
Assets	**Current**	**Goal**
Investment Property	£	£
Real estate (current equity)	£	£
Bonds	£	£
Stocks	£	£
Business net value	£	£
Credit cards (for good debt)	£	£
Available cash in bank	£	£
Other	£	£
Total Assets	£	£
Liabilities (necessities)	**Current**	**Goal**
Charity donations	£	
Taxes on total income	£	£
Home mortgage/rent	£	£
Credit cards (for bad debt)	£	£
Home running costs	£	£
Other	£	£
Total liabilities	£	£
Net worth Total assets—total liabilities	£	£

Analysis	Current	Goal
How much do you keep? Total cash flow—total expenses	£	£
How much do you pay in taxes? Total income taxes—total income	£	£
Does your money work hard for you? Portfolio & Passive incomes/ Total income	£	£
How much do you spend on expenses? Total expenses—total assets	£	£
What is your yearly return on assets? Passive & Portfolio incomes—Total assets	£	£

Becoming financially independent

Good debt is borrowing money to pay you more money than owed, whereas bad debt is costing you more money than you borrowed. The more your combination of assets that produces passive and portfolio income with decreasing liabilities and expenses, then the bigger your wealth and financial independence is.

Asset means Money into your pocket

An asset puts money into your pocket; an asset should generate income on a regular basis. The traditional definition of an asset is anything that you own is worth something and could be unlocked into money. Your assets also technically include the balance in any bank accounts in your name, or the current value stocks bonds that you have your wallet.

However, while you might consider your home, cars or expensive gadgets of value an "asset" it´s not really an asset until it is sold. Because it´s not putting any money into your pocket until then, and then it´s no longer an asset because it no longer belongs to you. Same thing goes for cash in your bank; your cash is not secretly reproducing itself by putting more money into your pocket. But there are places other than your wallet where cash reproduces itself by investing it in assets that give you a passive and portfolio income. Anything you own that produces passive or portfolio income is an asset.

Liabilities means Money out of your pocket

Liabilities are the opposite of assets. Liabilities cost money out of your pocket. Such as, the gadgets and cars like your TV or laptops that might traditionally be considered assets are currently liabilities, because it had cost money out of your pocket to get them. And many of them, when sold or loaned as cash, would give you back less money than you paid for them, because it depreciates in value. If the value of your home or your car, or business grows more than you pay for it, then it's still current liabilities that become asset when the value is released. Renting your home is a liability, because the landlord owns it and earns money from you.

A to Z

So you want to buy your first investment property? What happens next? What do you do? I meet a lot of people who decide it's time to start somewhere within property investment, but struggle to know what are all the steps, how to overcome the lack of finance, in which order and the most effective way. Some of you have been paying mortgage or renting your own home for a while, and some of you are buying in a changing market with changing rules.

1.   How much do you want to invest?

As with any investment that has the intention of giving you higher returns, there is a certain amount of risks involved. By getting clear about your property objectives, goals and carrying out due diligence and research, the risks can be limited.

From the outset, you need a certain amount of capital to work with and that amount will be a key determinant of your strategy. Working capital will ultimately be used to put down as a deposit, or to pay for professional services, such as surveyors, solicitors and builders. The more you can borrow from many of the varied sources, rather than only a bank, then the better. You are essentially using other people's money (OPM) to create profits and income to fund the lifestyle you want. This will also involve freeing up your time by using other people time (OPT) and other people's knowledge (OPK).

2.   Where do you want to buy?

This is probably the most important question out of all the important questions you need to ask yourself. The location of the property will have a massive effect on how many people want to rent and buy it if you want to sell.

3.   What sort of property are you going to buy?

Would it be the cheapest one or the one that you can afford? Is price going to be your only criteria? How much refurbishment will it need? Is it a wreck or a repossession that will needs a total do-over or can you make do with a cosmetic coat of paint? Are you looking for flats or 3 bedroom houses? Who are you going to let them out to? What will their resale value be? Have a think about these things, write down as much as your preferences as possible and consider the pros/cons via this book and discuss your ideas with a few people via Property networks and meetings. It's very important that you always buy at as deep a below market value as possible to expand the profit potential, so a minimum of 25% or more is recommended.

4.   What methods are you going to use to find your property?

There are a number of ways to advertise yourself and to contact those hard-to-find owners of houses that are or sale at over 25% below market value, such as newspaper adverts, cards in shop, advertise on specific property websites, use property sourcing agents and many more. When you are starting out, I would recommend starting via 'YourPropertyNetwork' magazines, property networks and property discussion websites.

5. Do a financial check and ensure the figures add up

There is no point in going into a financial transaction with a mortgage broker, a bank, a vendor, solicitors and your partners if the figures are incorrect. You are wasting their time and, more importantly, your own.

Find a decent finance broker or speak to your current mortgage provider and get your Decision In Principle (DIP) in writing before you start looking. If you have already got the finances in place when you find the ideal property, you can move swiftly up the pecking order when putting in an offer. If you are a cash buyer by using Other People's Money (OPM), then that is even better. Getting your funds and deposit in place before you start looking will speed the process up and will be one less thing to worry about when the purchasing process is set in motion.

Once you and the vendor agree to a price, stick to it and keep the negotiations simple. The only time you should consider backing out is if the survey report has thrown up some major problems which cost more than you budgeted. But don't make a habit of it, because you lose favour with the estate agent, if you are going through that route, or with potential vendors. There is a fine but distinctive line between investing firmly and being a timewaster.

6.   Get a survey done

If you are going to buy a house, getting a survey done is a form of insurance that will let you know if there is anything wrong with the property and, if so, what needs to be done about it. It will put you in the driving seat and you decide if you want to proceed with the sale. In most cases, the surveyors report will give you a bargaining tool to negotiate the price down further.

7.   Find your first tenant or buyer

Whist you are refurbishing your property or even giving it a lick of paint, you need to start advertising at the start and getting your tenant ready to move in. With credit checks and work references to follow up, this process can take anything between one to six weeks, so it's best to work on this process while the refurbishment is taking place. Don't wait until afterwards, because you have a month of paying the loan or mortgage fees with no rent coming in and the property is standing empty. Finding a good letting agent is also worthwhile, because they will do a huge amount of the work for you in exchange for around 10% of the rental income. Again, it's a case of using Other People's Time (OPT) and Other People's Knowledge (OPK).

If you are going to refurbish a property to sell at a profit, then consider advertising at the start, depending if it will take 2 weeks or halfway through if it will take 2 months. It's better to have potential buyers waiting to view or purchase the property, so you will have a surge of waiting potential buyers at the completion stage to negotiate with, quickly sell and move on.

8. Find a decent solicitor

There is a lot of legal paperwork to go through when buying a property and a decent solicitor is a wise investment, therefore ask around amongst the property investment community who is recommended. Take some time to interview a number of solicitors and see if they are on the same page as you, because a solicitor who will work efficiently and quickly for you is worth paying a premium for. Don't be afraid to be proactive with your solicitor and keep in regular contact with them, and feel free to chase them if you have to, but if you pick the right solicitor, you shouldn't have to do too much chasing.

9. Exchange of contracts

Once you are happy with everything, the survey report is in and any negotiations have taken place from its findings and the legal searches have been completed and agreed, then it's time to exchange contracts. This usually takes place between 7 and 14 days before completion, although exchange and completion can take place on the same day. However, if you decide to back out after exchange of contracts, you will lose your deposit. In some cases, you may be able to do the refurbishment between exchange of contracts and completion, therefore you won't make any mortgage payments until you have got your tenants in and they are paying the mortgage for you.

10. Do the refurbishment

Many property investors are builders who want to take on projects while their own work is slow, or just to have extra work on their spare time, but since the economic market changed in 2008, the building industry have struggled as projects decrease. This is a good thing for you as a property investor, because you can negotiate the cost of refurbishment with them, especially if you are going to give them regular work. But if the refurbishment is just a lick of paint and you have the time, then you can do that yourself. While this is going on, keep a tab and a lid on your costs and ensure they don't spiral out of control, because you want your property to be a money provider, not a money pit.

11. Set your finances up

Have a separate bank account for your property expenses and rental income, it will be easier to administrate and set up direct debits where necessary so that the mortgage and insurances are paid on time automatically. If you are selling at the new higher market value after refurbishments after you have re-value it, you can refinance it to reinvest into another property. You should have a significant amount of capital from it if you have bought it below market value.

CAPITAL GAINS

1. The gross capital gain percentage:

Deduct the purchase cost from the sales proceeds to get a capital gain, by calculating your entire capital gain percentage figure and express this gain as a percentage of your investment. If you have fixed yourself a percentage target to accomplish, use that target as the tool when determining which properties to buy, and those that make the score, get moved onto to be further evaluated. Those properties that don't make the score are removed from your potential purchasing pool.

a) Imagine a property costs: £10,000 or £1,000,000
b) You sell it for: £12,000 or £1,200,000
c) Making a capital gain of £2,000 or £200,000

Which is stated as a percentage of the cost of £10,000 (a) is:
£2,000 (c) / £10,000 (a) x 100 = 20%

Also, exactly the same 20% percentage applies for £1,000,000:
£200,000 / £1,000,000 x 100 = 20%

If you have fixed your target gain at 19% or less, this property would be further evaluated, and if your target is set at 21% or more, it would be removed. There is always plenty more out there that will meet your target percentage, so don't accept anything less. Also, if you are adopting this method, you could settle your capital gain target as a relative to your cost of capital. Therefore, if you borrow money at 20%, you may assume that anything over 20% is desirable, but you could consider targeting your potential gain to be, such as, double your cost of capital.

   2.   The gross return including the entire cost of refurbishment:

If you are buying to refurbish to resell, you will need to include all the costs of renovation.

   a)   Imagine a property costs: £120,000
   b)   You spend on refurbishment: £30,000
   c)   You sell it for: £190,000
   d)   Making a capital gain of: £40,000

Which is stated as a percentage of the total cost of £150,000 (a+b) is: £40,000 (d)/ £150,000 (a+b) x 100 = 26%

For calculation purposes, consider if 26% scores your target or not, therefore your decision is easily defined.

As part of your calculation tool kit, it's essential to develop a complete refurbishment cost control list. Remember to agree for costs and include a cost for the time needed to renovate throughout that time: allow for the water taxes, service charges, mortgage, council and other costs in your calculation.

   3.   Cash flow technique on capital purchases:

The financially calculated question you need to ask is "could I afford to support it?", if you are adopting a strategy to invest in your property for capital growth. In this situation, you list all the expenses giving you a monthly cash outflow figure. Input this outlay figure into your normal monthly budgeted expenditure just like the costs of a home you lived in.

Remember to include the possible costs:

- Council tax
- Water standing charges
- Basis gas and or electricity standing charges
- Telephone
- General maintenance and repairs
- Mortgages
- Insurances

You could form the main costs as illustrated above or edit for your own personal situations and trial each cost by doing a sensitivity analysis with this and play the 'what if' scenario for precaution:

- How much would your situations have to adjust, before the investment becomes a financial burden, if it isn't profitable enough? Such as getting divorced, resigning or losing your backup job, having your first or another child, etc.
- If you suddenly inherit or win a lot of money, would the investment still work?
- If the interest rate increase by 2%, or 3% or even 9% would the investment still work?
- How much would the interest rate have to increase before the investment no longer works?

- If there is anything such as the roof needing a sudden replacement, is there enough gain in the property to afford a sizeable credit?
- If you want a managing agent looking after the property, would the investment still work?

The closing questions would be the most relevant, because it ensures you really test the success of the investment in relations of the strategy and the longer duration position. The type of answers you have to consider, if you ask yourself these questions:

- Paying off this mortgage immediately, this could indicate a lack of assurance in the original investment strategy.
- Still keeping the property investment, yet using the inheritance for other things, which could indicate the success of the original investment decision and its relevance.
- Using the inheritance to get out the investment completely, possibly you have had the strategy incorrect in the first place.
- Accept that there is no better purpose or better return than the property investment, thus approving the original investment decision.

Income

Obviously, you have got some target assumed for income generation with income strategies, so what would that be?

A few of the following ways to calculate income is:

1. Cash flow foundation

In this calculation you just take all the inflows and deduct all the outflows to see what is left.

Monthly:

Inflow: Rental income =

Outflows:

- Gas and safety checks =
- Management fees =
- Insurances =
- Funding costs =
- Other costs =

Net cash inflow/outflow =

Ensure that you include the costs that are applicable to your investment strategy when you are calculating in this method. Imagine if you are managing all your investment properties yourself, including finding tenants, collecting rents, thus you ignore the cost of an allowance for any management fees. However, if the property is too far away from you and you never plan to visit, you will need to have all the management offered and clearly you need to share a far greater proportion of costs to its management.

Also, there is typically a higher charge for student type properties than professional let and they differ across the country, so it's vital to check specific management fees. Remember, that the more properties you own, the stronger your negotiating power would be with agents.

Consider how this particular investment fits into the rest of your property investment portfolio, if you own several properties. If you prefer your properties to be cash positive completely, therefore you may be able to include properties that could be cash positive at a later stage, since somewhere else in the portfolio there is another property that produces enough monthly cash to balance the temporary losses on other properties.

The other considered costs will vary from strategy to strategy and from person to person. You can obtain a maintenance contracts for everything that you will need, such as, redecorating normal gas, electricity maintenance, plumbing, cleaning, gas boiler annual checks and carpet cleaning etc. To reduce your monthly cash flow for all these things, one method would be including all the costs of maintenance contracts. Alternatively, you could willingly take the hit of precise costs when they occur if you prefer.

You can alter your evaluation accordingly to suit you, when recognising what the right level of cash flow is for you and for your individual strategy.

Ensure you can insure everything that is related with rental properties, and you may prefer to insure against void periods.

2. Gross return basis

This is an effective and easy method which takes your gross return as a percentage of the purchase cost as follows:

Imagine the rent of £1,500 monthly, so £1,500 x 12 months, equates to: £1,500 x 12 months = £18,000

Imagine the property cost: £150,000

Take: £18,000 / £150,000 x 100: 12%

Take the monthly rent x 12 months: Annual rent.

Take the annual rent / purchase price x 100: Gross return yearly

You can test yourself questions with this gross return such as:

- What else could I do with the money that may produce over 12%? Don't invest in the property if you have several other opportunities with higher percentage; otherwise you can continue to calculate the property confidently.
- What is the cost of funding that you have to pay when investing in this property? If it's less than 12% then it look optimistic, otherwise ask yourself questions if the property is right for you?

Use this method to compare one possible investment against another, to calculate the best property for you, therefore as a minimum, try practicing with this type of method and you soon get accustomed with calculations.

3. Net annual profit basis

You can calculate this method which provides you with a net profit or loss percentage begin by taking the cash inflows minus the outflows, which results in a remaining monthly balance. Then, to get a yearly profit figure, you multiply that by 12 months. To get the net yearly profit, you express that figure as a percentage of the gross income.

Monthly:

Rental income inflow = £

Outflows =

- Funding costs =
- Tax =
- Other monthly costs =

    Net monthly inflow/outflow =

Multiply this net figure by 12 to get an annual profit.

Take the annual profit and divide it by the gross annual rent (the rental income x 12 months) and then multiply by 100.

This results in an annual profit percentage.

Imagine the annual inflow is £9,000, and the annual rental is £18,000 (£1,500 x 12 months). Therefore, your annual profit percentage is:

£9,000 / £18,000 x 100 = 50%

This will give you a figure that you can calculate against other property investment opportunities.

Ensure that you completely contain all the costs you may incur, as these will vary for each property and will depend on your personal level of input to the management of the properties.

4.   Return on cash invested or cash on cash invested

This is possibly the most typical method of calculating the property investments, when it's calculated by taking the net cash inflow, as above, and stating that as a percentage of the quantity of money you have invested in the property. Basically, you are mainly concerned in what return you get on your money, but this calculation method is irrelevant if you have done a 'no money down' deal.

So if the net inflow is £9,000 on a property costing £200,000 and you have put down a 10% deposit of £10,000, the calculation is: £9,000 / £10,000 x 100 = 45%

Furthermore, the questions you make at this point are similar: How does this compare to other property investments? What better purpose do you have for the money?

Nevertheless, after you have complete these calculations numerous times, you become so swift and skilled, that you make the calculations swiftly and in your notepad habitually as you are viewing the properties. Use any available blank forms to create a simple and swift system of property valuation, and also, construct a property review pack, which has as many of these calculation methods as you wish to use.

BOOST YOUR INCOME WITH HMOS

An HMO is a House of Multiple Occupation and is a property which is separated into several units. It can be a property with four bedrooms which is shared by four nurses, or it can be an 11 bedroom property which is separated into 11 bedsits for students. Two unrelated people sharing are excluded from the term HMO, because that is flatmate.

- Students living in united accommodation where they have exclusive use of the whole house
- An owner-occupier with more than 2 lodgers who have a licence to live in their accommodation
- A house divided into bedsits where the tenant has private use of their room but shares a kitchen or bathroom.
- A house or flat share with 3 or more tenants who are unrelated to each other

The term can also refer to hostels for vulnerable individuals, bed and breakfast accommodation or hotels that are perhaps used for homeless people, women's refuges, night shelters etc, but these categories aren't relevant to most residential landlords, therefore an HMO is any property which have several tenants and which is occupied by a non standard family unit. If you are unsure about anything, check very carefully with your local HMO office, which you can find at the local Housing Office. To find this, ask at the local library, or Citizens Advice office.

There are individual regulations, such as fire safety and security, which governs HMOs, which you need to comply with that you don't need in the same way for normal buy to let properties, therefore get a copy of the regulations and ensure that you understand what you are getting into here.

If you have the time and energy to battle the red tape here, the returns can be very high. Instead of receiving one rent such as, £800 monthly for your 4 bedrooms house, you could get 4 sources of £300 resulting in £1,200 monthly from the 4 nurses, by separating the property up and charge by the room instead of charging for a whole property. You also have the advantage of using properties which wouldn't let as a house and are often cheaper to buy than a house of the same size as an HMO, such as an old mansion or offices. The rent received by doing this can be as much as three times the rent accomplished letting the property as a complete to one tenant. Although, there is usually a big administration and regulations involved when letting an HMO property, it can still be financially worthwhile.

HMOs can be a huge income generator, but as usual, do your researches completely before you adopt this strategy.

Be very precise:

You need to be very precise with your strategy and buy the correct property for the proposed tenant, because a house for 4 sharing nurses differs fairly to a house full of unconnected students. You need to consider how they live and what that means in terms of bathrooms and kitchens, communal areas, property layout and room size. If you are unsure how students and nurses live, just ask a letting agent to show you around a few potential properties and you will soon learn.

Location:

Students, nurses and anybody who needs to live in an HMO, needs to be reasonably close to where they need to study and work, as they are unlikely to have their own transport. Therefore these properties need to be only a few streets away from the college campus, or the hospital or suitable amenities.

Be legally safe:

You need to take further care with the tenancy agreement, any house sharing agreement, and arranging references. You can never be too careful by asking for parental guarantees in the case of young people and students, so ensure that you secure as much as possible.

There is a new Section 257 HMOs category where many Councils have yet to take action to improve these properties, which constitute a considerable proportion of the housing stock. A section 257 HMO is a building converted into flats (self contained) that was converted prior to the 1991 Building Regulations and still does not meet those standards, because it may have been converted without permission. The defining aspect is that at least a third of the flats are rented out on short tenancies, e.g. let on a short-hold assured tenancy and unoccupied solely by leaseholders. If you own a flat or live in a flat in a building like these, then you do need to install better fire safety measures (smoke detection in the common areas) and you are subject to specific management regulations. This would be done in co-operation with your fellow leaseholders and the management company. Since April 2010, a new planning use class of HMO was enacted called C4 that qualifies 3 or more people sharing as a minimum as opposed to a minimum of 6.

It's important to understand what an HMO is so that you can decide if you require additional fire safety measures or an HMO licence. You should always speak to one of their officers or check the website of your Council to check what rules apply locally. The main rules that apply to all housing in the UK are contained in the Housing Act 2004 and the regulations made under it. This Act brought in HMO licensing and tightened up the law on the definition of an HMO so all those affected could be clear about this type of housing. The Act also set out a new way of risk assessing housing (the Housing Health and Safety Rating system), which looks at the health effects of poor housing and the potential harm that can be caused. It's vital that you find out from your local Council what planning policies apply. How the rules are applied is very much dependant on the local plan and enforcement policies so do check the website or call in to see your Planning Officer, also, many Councils operate a planning duty desk or drop-in counter. The effects of contravening planning law can be severe and costly so do check first. If you do need to make an application there is a planning fee, depending on your Council's charging policy.

- Safety measures—Fire escapes and detection systems in good order and repair; protection from injury (falls from balconies, windows etc).
- Water supply and drainage—water supply to be maintained and protected from frost; tanks and cisterns to be covered.

- Gas and electricity—gas and electricity supplies to be maintained; gas safety certificates to be available for inspection; electrical tests every 5 years.
- Common parts, fixtures, fittings and appliances—all common areas (such as staircases, passageways, corridors and entrances) are kept reasonably free from obstruction, maintained in good and clean decorative repair and in safe working condition. Included are gas and electricity supplies, lighting and heating/hot water
- Living accommodation—each letting room to be in good order and maintained as such and clean at the beginning of the tenancy.
- Lighting, windows and ventilation—All windows and ventilation to be kept in good repair. Common areas to have adequate lighting.
- Outbuildings in common use—All outbuildings, walls and outside spaces to be repaired, kept clean and not a danger.
- Garden to be safe and tidy.
- Waste disposal facilities—enough bins to be provided and storage for refuse prior to collection.
- Information to occupiers—The name, addresses and telephone contact number of the manager must be made available to each occupier and the details clearly displayed in a prominent position in the house.
- Duties of occupiers—It's the duty of all residents of an HMO to ensure that the manager can effectively carry out his duties. All residents must allow access, provide information, comply with refuse arrangements,

be of good conduct, take care of fixtures and fittings, comply with instructions about fire safety, and treat premises in a tenant-like manner.

There will be a fee for the licence (which lasts for five years). You will need to prove your management arrangements, that you are a fit and proper person and that the HMO is in good order. The CLG website has full details of the mandatory licensing scheme via www.communities.gov.uk/publications/housing/hmolicensingguide

No money down deals

No money down deals is when you can buy a property without any of your own money, therefore they are mainly deals when you arrange the financing and it can happen with different alterations. When you read about the no money down deals, you find that the huge majority of the structures demonstrated are methods of handling of some kind of personal debt, and they are in the main credit card arrangements. Some types of deals suit different strategies, such as those adopting the no money down at the beginning, or those who can arrange some starting capital providing you a head start. These are useful methods if you don't have any money to start with, also payments may eventually have to be made; but usually financial outlay can be deferred for many years until other cash/wealth has been created.

Some of the many ways of securing no money down deals are:

- You use one or more of your credit card to refill the mortgage the purchase amount.
- You use your family asset as the deposit for the property, but importantly the seller must agree to receive an asset other than money as a deposit.
- You arrange a 100% seller financing method.
- You achieve a personal loan, or overdraft in combination with a mortgage.
- You arrange a gifted deposit from the seller and get a mortgage for the rest.
- You organise a 85% BTL mortgage with OPM for the deposit.
- You achieve 100% funding for a property from a mixture of a mortgage or seller financing.

The three main types of no money deals are:

- No money down ever deals.
- No money down for the current time deals; which begins without money, until you have created money finally.
- No money down finally deals; which begin with own money, then recover it all with increased money finally.

No money down finally deals:

Imagine you use a property-sourcing agent who works in a specific area of the country where properties are less expensive or you could source particular properties yourself to save money, if you have the time and effort. So if in reality the capital growth opportunities are not as high as they might be in other parts of the country, but the income potential is high and fairly secure. The agent sources a property that is 'distressed' and needs development, therefore the property is being sold at BMV (below market value). You purchase the property and renovate it, but it depends on the severity of the 'distress' stat of the property, because for the best efficiency, the type of renovation needed has to be cosmetic only. Although, structural damage may work financially and may create sufficient returns, however it demands so much time to complete the work with more risks involved. On the other hand, if you want to do this strategy on structurally distressed properties, ensure you include more time required in your calculations. Finally, after achieving a revaluation on the completed refurbishment of the property, you advertise it well and sell it for more than the price you bought it for, thus giving you a capital gain.

An illustration:

Imagine when you acquire a property, refurbish it and then remortgage it at a higher value; therefore withdrawing all of your original investment finally. Imagine you purchase a distressed property for £100,000 using a 70% LTV (loan to value), £70,000 mortgage and a £30,000 loan. Then spend another £10,000 refurbishing the property using credit cards. Then, when the property is looking good, return to the finance provider and request for a revaluation. Therefore, the revaluation is at £180,000, so you apply for a new mortgage at the higher re-valued amount, and at 70% LTV (Loan to value), now they provide a mortgage of £126,000. It's now possible to repay the original loan of £70,000 and have £56,000 available to clear the loan debt of £30,000 (used for the deposit) and the £10,000 refurbishment costs, whilst having £16,000 available. Even though there is money invested throughout, this deal has been completed with no money down finally.

If you plan to adopt this form of refurbishment strategy, ensure you organise the original finance with the revaluation in mind. Some finance providers do this favourably, some will only revalue after a certain period and some completely disapprove. If this is a main share of your strategy, prepare some questions about their approach for revaluations at an early stage.

Lastly, imagine after spending £10,000 refurbishing a distressed property you purchased for £60,000; after 5 months it gets a revaluation for £120,000. Therefore, you arrange a mortgage for £84,000 which is 70% of LTV, then you receive you initial outlay of £60,000, your costs of £10,000 plus £14,000 as a contribution to your expenses. Additionally, you now own 30% in a property that you didn't have before.

<u>No money down for the current time deals:</u>

It's useful using credit cards as no money down for the current time method, because these are increasingly common and offers you flexibility when you know how to manage and use it for its full potential. When searching online and in credit card papers, you can view, analyse and compare for credit cards in mass ways. You can choose those that have 0% n balance transfers, those with 0% interest for an agreed period, those with annual fees and those without any annual fees. There are so many choices and types of credit cards for different situations or strategies, so you may find some suitable types for yourself.

Obviously, it's easier if you own credit cards that'll give you

- — 0% on new purchases
- — Credit card cheques
- — 0% interest on balance transfers

It's also better to get the 0% on balance transfers for as long as possible, such as the usual 6 months period or so. However, it's possible and it exists, that some credit card companies lengthen this period much longer, even 0% balance transfer rate for the entirety of the balance life. Understandably, if these are ordinary credit cards, there will be interest growing, but only if you fail to repay the payment on time and in full amount. Be alert to ensure all the credit cards payments are fulfilled to continue the pattern, so careful timing and planning is vital, otherwise you may have to pay some interest. Careful choice of credit cards is crucial to this specific strategy too.

An illustration:

Imagine you have applied and received two credit cards, where one is a Visa and the other is a MasterCard. You have hired a sourcing agent or sourced a property you are planning to purchase for £70,000. So you obtain a mortgage such as 90% of LTV which is £65,000. This method has other bonuses such as improving your credit rating, because you are repaying on time and in full amount. You also get into a habit which gives you confidence knowing how it works.

1. You put the balance of £5,000 on the Visa credit card, now the Visa card company informs and requests their £5,000 back 29 days or so later.

2. At this stage, you have prepared a cheque from MasterCard to pay £5,000 to the Visa card Company.

3. You have cleared the Visa card balance.

4. After putting the £5,000 balance onto the MasterCard to repay the Visa card, you are given another 29 days or so.

5. You have cleared the MasterCard balance and the pattern can continue if you need more time.

Basically, the £5,000 deposit which is not your own money can be used in swing motion between both credit cards and you can do this until you can afford to repay it all off with a gain, or arrange a revaluation on the property at an increased value so the new 90% mortgage provides enough money to repay the £5,000 off. You could also use numerous credit cards, and if you are in the process of increasing your credit rating to qualify for credit cards, you could ask your family/partners credit cards to adopt this method for you. Bear in mind, most credit card companies are familiar with this method and pattern, so check if they even automatically transfer the money in swing motion for your conveniences.

Another illustration:

The other type of this is to take 6 months interest free credit on cards A and B, so when their 6 months balance life is fulfilled, apply for credit card C and D and take advantage of another 6 months interest free credit. Again, this pattern can continue if you require more time. However, if your credit card gives you a direct interest free period for six months, you can leave the deposit on that card for the entire six months; then go in swing motion to move the balance to an additional card.

Whilst you have two credit cards where one gives you credit card cheques as most does, and one that gives you an interest free period on balance transfers such as 6 months; you can use the credit card cheque to fund the deposit on the property and when the credit card payment is due, then transfer the balance onto the card with 0% interest balance transfers. There may still be a small fee to pay for the credit card cheque itself, but the effect will be tiny, if you clear the balance by the due date. Therefore, by careful preparation of exchange and timing such as due dates, you can maximise the credit free periods and available credit. So even on a one month cycle, the due date may be anything up to 56 days away, so choose your completion dates carefully to gain that added month of interest freedom.

Some finance providers refuse loans or mortgages for below £25,000, and some allow it, so if you are considering this strategy and you are interested in remortgaging on the increased value afterward, then consider evaluating if the re-valued amount will be £25,000 or above. Alternatively, find a finance provider who will work below £25,000.

Although, the simple strategy of buy, repair and revalue, is interesting, this method can be the starting point in a selection of property investment strategies.

- Consider the income opportunity of each managed properties that may produce a consistent income. So, if you have a tenant in each property once you purchased it, you could receive £120 weekly in rental income. This equates to £520 monthly, which would roughly be £356 per month, if the mortgage is £80,000. On these rough calculations, individually these properties could generate over £164 monthly income.

- Consider withdrawing the money after completion of your first refurbishment to reinvest into another property, and then another, and another. Shortly, you own 30% of many properties, or a different percentage depending on the mortgage you get.

So, basically imagine you have made an original investment of £60,000 intended to purchase numerous properties, all producing net cash in flow of approximately £164 monthly. Although, you have borrowed the original £25,000 on a personal loan, you will still be cash positive after all, and you be gathering self-funding assets, at whatever speed you required.

The same £60,000 can be continually rolled over until you want to cease acquiring properties. On the other hand, you own a collection of income generating assets that you have grown, that someone else such as the tenants have paid for; if you leave these properties to mature at small rates of capital growth yearly, for the complete 25 years of the mortgage, or even by your retirement time.

You can create a fantastic property investment portfolio, when considering two or more of the strategies above together. With the added advantages of the original investment being on the credit card swing system, it's possible to adapt the strategy above which is rolled over the same original investment into a succession of properties. So you accumulate properties that somebody else funds from monthly rental income, and the whole portfolio is gained with no money down.

Case study:

My friends Thomas and Emma from Kent considered investing in property investments in 2008 for a while, but they expected it will be impossible to start in the midst of a different property market where mortgages were much stricter and limited. They knew I was a property investor and asked me what to do and where to begin, so I decided to mentor them at no cost with plenty of advice for them via Skype and calls whilst I was investing. They felt discouraged when they explained they had no money of their own to use, with no jobs to depend on, no credit cards, but they were very curious about property investing. They wanted to invest in property when they heard how strong the rental demand was rising with so many properties being repossessed and available at huge discounts. They decided that they must be an alternative way to overcome the financial obstacles.

However, with more available time and effort due to their unemployment, they attended, listened and discussed with other successful property investors at property networks, free seminars and listened to audio books. I explained about the no money downs deals that they didn't know existed and how it could work for them. They also took the opportunity at the networks to find recommended local solicitors who were familiar with working for property investors with minimal time, who could handle the sale and purchase processes within 2 days. They felt more encouraged to try this creative strategy and laid out a few plans to ensure it will work.

Their No Money Down strategy with an exit plan was very effective, because:

1. They wrote down all the obstacles such as how they had no money, no incomes, poor credit ratings and living at their parents in their 30s. Then they discussed and weighted the pros and cons of each type of the available solutions and alternatives that would suit their needs and these were completely new to them.

2. They explored and practised analysing the potentiality of many BMV properties from various sources such as auctions, property magazines and specialised websites. They decided what their minimum targets are, listed as many possible finance sources, and practised how and why others should invest in them. They understood it was vital to have money prepared when a suitable property appeared, because the quicker and easier the purchase process was, then the deeper the discounts on the properties will be.

3. They realised that both their parents have mortgages on their home and confirmed a considerable equity

of £75,000 was available to invest with, so Thomas and Emma explained what they planned to do if they invested in them and what the returns could be on some property examples they have financially analysed. The parents began the paperwork to release the equity, and if more money was needed, a guarantor loan and the credit cards could be used as a financial contingency plan. A legal agreement was offered for the parents to safeguard the money and outline the details, such as of how much in minimum of profit could be discovered and when it will all be repaid.

Even if their parents didn't have or refused to release any equity by remortgaging the properties, one of the many possibilities was they could seek JV partners available at numerous property networks and magazines, ensuring everyone can benefit from a profitable project.

4. They began advertising in a few newspapers covering Kent as they thought it would give the best response and the most direct publicity. They didn't need to hire a call answering service, because they didn't have jobs to preoccupy so much of their time and they prepared a list of questions to ask the motivated sellers to assess the property's financial suitability. Even if the equity release process took 6 weeks, instead of letting time cost them money, they had a contingency plan to sell the qualified leads found from the motivated sellers and sell it onwards to other property investors via specialised sourcing websites. This would give

them between 1% and 4% of the property's purchase price instantly to build cash reserves and this could provide the deposit for a BTL mortgage.

5. Within a week of advertising in one of the local newspapers, they received a call from a lady about selling her property as soon as possible. Thomas asked about her situation and discovered that her reason for selling was due to dwindling pension and needed to relocate closer to her family in a bungalow quickly. Thomas took this opportunity to arrange a visit to assess her property and discuss how they could help her with a win/win solution.

6. Prior to visiting the property, Thomas and Emma did their research and found the property was already being advertised by an estate agent at a significantly reduced price of £110,000. Similar properties on the street were being advertised at £150,000 to £160,000 and checked the previous sold prices in the area and this confirmed them that the property was greatly reduced. At this time, the equities of £75,000 were released, with £5,000 available credit from the parents and a guarantor loan of £10,000, totalling £85,000 available cash ready to invest with.

7. When Thomas met the lady at the property, she explained her situation and how it was important to move forward quickly and he assured her that the deal would proceed as agreed. Meanwhile he took this visit as an opportunity check the property properly, it had 4 double bedrooms, 2 en-suite bathrooms with

upstairs shared bathroom, a guest toilet downstairs and an open plan dining room. The décor needed a minor cosmetic updating, and the back garden was low maintenance and spacious. It was situated in a convenient location just 10 minutes walk into town with a major bus and train station. This would make an ideal HMO that could generate £300 per room which is a total of £1,200 monthly gross rental income, instead of £900 monthly income as a family home. The rental demand in the area was strong and they checked the rent for similar multi-let properties was between £250 and £300.

8. Thomas and the lady decided that to sell her property within 2 days, he could purchase it for £80,000 instead of waiting for buyers in a weak property market with the risks of buyers pulling out and mortgage paperwork delaying the process. She agreed with this arrangement and was pleased to finally move on with her life; Thomas and Emma were also pleased to find a heavily discounted property with huge financial potential. The parents were satisfied for receiving a regular agreement of interest from the leftover rental income, after the repayments was being covered creating a win/win deal. The sale was processed within 3 days with the help of a solicitor who is familiar at exchanging contracts and completing paperwork promptly. Their parents were updated on the process, because a huge amount of money was being carefully invested, so an open and honest communication was vital and the repayments were taken care of.

The summary of this deal is:

- They used other people's money (OPM) for the purchase, necessary legal fees and minor cosmetic update.

- The true market value of the property was £155,000 with an agreed purchase price of £80,000 (47% BMV) which is £75,000 instant available equity if they decide to sell it.

- After realising it is more tax efficient to release the equity with a new mortgage, they agreed to let the property out as multi-let (with a required HMO licence) to cover all the repayments and purchase another investment property.

Now this is just one of the 12 extra properties they have purchased since 2008 and they have also sold numerous qualified leads to other property investors, because these properties didn't meet their minimum ROI criteria, which made them over £37,000. They now have a passive net rental income of £8,400 monthly and continue to ensure their team boost their property portfolio, ensuring they have more financial security and freedom to spend their time with loved ones.

Seller Financing

The purpose of seller financing, in its simplest form, is when the seller allows some of the money for you to buy their property, although some people appear to make this issue unnecessarily difficult. There are people and occasions when sellers are willing, and even offer to put up some money for you, providing it will be beneficial for both sides. This method occurs daily and countless times, even many people have built up their whole property portfolio worth up to multi-millions, simply by acquiring properties from sellers who agree the finance. It's especially common with very knowledgeable and advanced property owners, providing themselves an easier way of regular income or pension.

An illustration:

If you have no money of your own at all, but you want to purchase a property for £100,000, therefore you arrange an 80% mortgage. You will still need the £20,000 which could be obtained as a personal loan, or an overdraft from your bank, or borrow from family/friends. So when you have negotiated to borrow £20,000 from your seller, this is essentially seller financing in its simplest form, because you have return to the seller, asking to borrow the additional £20,000 from them. The point of this example is regardless of whether the loan is 70% or up to 90% LTV (Loan to value) on a £100,000 property, you could get the rest of the fund from the seller as a seller financing method.

In this occasion, the seller would lend you £20,000 and you repay them over an agreed time, rate, and amount per weekly, monthly or quarterly. You repay the seller in precisely the same way you repay your overdraft, personal loan, family or friend. You get the property and the seller gets two things, which is a motivated buyer for their property and secondly they get a better rate of interest from you as a purchaser on the £20,000, instead of it sitting in the bank. Therefore, there are plenty of sellers who willingly seek these kinds of deals as a way of making a gain or income on the money. If your seller has never used this reliable method before, you explain how it's beneficial for both sides and the funds should be legally protected ensuring it will be repaid on agreeable terms.

In the same previous method, the seller can provide all of the financing for a change, so instead of getting a mortgage at any LTV on a property worth £100,000, you basically take ownership of the property, and then repay the seller at a legally agreed rate over a duration and amount. So you repay your monthly loan or 'mortgage' to the seller, instead of the finance company. In this situation, you negotiated a complete seller financing, and the added advantage is you have also taken ownership of this property, without putting any of your own money into the deal such as deposits and mortgage costs.

Furthermore, if you are a seller with very good credit rating and you can borrow the full or portion of easily at low interest rates money or use your own capital, it's a profitable idea to borrow money cheaply in order to loan money to other people at higher rates. The seller normally gets either a second mortgage as a security, but ensure you check with your primary lender that they are happy with second charges, or a personal loan contract. You are aiming to earn more in agreed repayment charges from the buyer to cover the lower loan repayments itself, ensuring you have an additional income whilst ensuring you have a motivated buyer for your property.

After you have both discussed and approved everything, it's vital that you and the buyer have a bookkeeping file or record to ensure an agreed regular date, the agreed repayment amount expected. Ensure a legal contract has been made for reliability and safety of funds, and set up a direct debit for ease and security.

- Would it be repaid weekly, monthly or quarterly?
- What is the repayment amount?
- What is the percentage of interest rate?
- How long is the loan?
- Have you ensured you will always be able to repay it?
- Have you discussed, decided and secured your agreements as a legal contract to protect you both financially?

Reversionary

This is technically called a 'sales and leaseback' arrangement, so it's a property reversion where the seller releases the capital in their home. This is a method of equity release for usually older people who either want a lump sum or a regular income, which they obtain by selling their home at a substantial discount. In return, they get the right to live in it for as long as they want for, generally, no rent. There are two types of reversionary properties: tenanted and untenanted. Tenanted is when the seller stays in the property, while untenanted is when the seller isn't residing in the property and the buyer can choose to rent out the property.

There are companies that specifically offer reversionary solutions, because 98% of the population will die poor, because we are all living longer. That means everyone will need more money to support them into their old age and it is unlikely that the state will be able to afford to support them. Not even the company pension schemes can be completely relied on. Therefore there will be a growing increase of people motivated to sell their properties at huge discounts, to avoid working beyond the normal retirement age and also avoid living a lower standard in their old age.

When payment has been handed over, the homeowner continues to reside in the property as a rent-free tenant with full legal rights to stay in the house. As long as he continues to stay in the house, he will be responsible for the general maintenance of the property, the utility bills, building insurance premiums and capital tax. Basically, reversion investments are a bet on the life expectancy of the homeowner. Meanwhile, the buyer of the property pays the monthly reversionary annuities until the death of the seller, because when he or she dies or decides to leave, the property's ownership reverts to you as the buyer. The reversionary property presents an excellent opportunity to acquire a property at a huge discount. Most of these reversionary properties are apartments, studio flats, villas and commercial buildings situated in prime spots thus making them well-suited for buy to lets.

A reversionary property investment is certainly one of the most convenience ways for any property investor to invest. The property is sold for huge discounts, normally about 40%—50% of open market value, at wholesale prices. These deals can be arranged privately through reputable agencies.

Advantages:

- **Higher Return Rate.** The buyer usually receives a higher rate of return in a sale-leaseback than in a conventional loan arrangement. Also, you may be able to avoid state usury laws that limit the rate of interest charged with conventional financing. In addition, at the end of the lease term, you receive the benefit of any appreciation in the value of the property. Finally, you can leverage the purchase with mortgage financing; this may further magnify the return rate on the cash invested.

- **Predictable and Secure Return Rate.** The long-term net lease enables the buyer to estimate accurately the expected future rate of return. Also, the extended term of the lease provides you with protection from downturns in the real estate market and an inflation hedge, assuming that the property value appreciates over time.

- **Ownership of the Reversion.** You own the reversionary interest in the property. If the seller has an option to purchase or an option to renew the lease, this may limit or postpone the time that the buyer actually realizes the profit potential. You also bear the risk that the property value actually might decline over the lease term.

- **Greater Ease in Handling a Seller Default.** In the event that the seller defaults under the lease, you can simply terminate the lease and have the seller evicted. The risk here is that you may have trouble finding another tenant after the eviction process is completed.

- **Avoid Loaning Problems.** In a sale-leaseback arrangement, you can avoid the state loaning problems encountered by lenders when money is tight. You and the seller can establish any mutually agreed upon rent level.

- **Built-in Tenant.** Finally, in purchasing the property, you have a built-in tenant, namely the seller.

Disadvantages

- **Possibility of Seller Default.** Perhaps the biggest risk that you face is that the seller will default on the lease, which would leave you without a tenant. If the seller files for bankruptcy, you are considered a general creditor. If the arrangement were a conventional mortgage, you would be considered a secured creditor. If the seller files for bankruptcy in a low rental demand market, you may have a difficult time finding a new tenant.

– **Higher Administrative Costs.** Because the typical sale-leaseback usually must be structured to meet the specific needs and requirements of both parties, it may require more time and increased administrative costs than a conventional loan transaction.

– **Required Property Management.** In most cases, the seller assumes the responsibility and expense of day-to-day property management during the lease term. However, you must ensure that the seller pays the property taxes on time and that tax assessments are reviewed and challenged when appropriate. You must also periodically review the insurance coverage on the property and inspect it for proper maintenance.

Overall, both the seller and you as the buyer benefit from a reversionary property. The homeowner-seller receives additional income in the form of a cash lump sum or monthly payments which could significantly supplement his/her pension. The setup will also provide a lease that will endure until they pass away and will be freed from the responsibility of shelling out big payments such as land tax. In addition, they don't have to put up with the usual anxiety associated with selling their own property or moving out, allowing them a stable and secure state of mind.

Momentum

This straightforward and systematic strategy involves reaping some significant rewards if it all goes to plan, if you adopt a much defined calculated model to unlock thousands in return percentage on your money within 20 years. Does 20 years sound too long to wait? 20 years will soon fly quickly and it can even be shorten to 10 years if you prefer. It's a method that anybody can do, but it's not for those expecting a 'get rich quick' opportunity and it's easy if you understand what you are doing. Even if you wish to continue working full or part time in your job, and prefer to adopt this strategy with minimal time, you can still create serious long term wealth. Having an alternative short term monthly income will be practical, because this strategy will do very little to add to your short term monthly income, but having your mortgages paid off by your tenants will create significant wealth over the long term.

Needless to say, property can be a very expensive business when things backfire, therefore in the event of large unforeseen repair bills, this strategy is unlikely to be suited to those with very modest incomes, or without the capital reserves, or access to cash to pay the bills if things potentially backfires. It really helps to have an approach ensuring each deals fit your stringent criteria to enable you to succeed with this method. This approach may not be exciting and fast, or suitable for replacing your day job or short term income, but it's a concrete and reliable choice for those seeking a long term financial goal whilst minimising the risks.

How does it work?

You gradually buy a total 20 relatively high yield properties (around 8-10% gross return) and stick them on a 20 year repayment mortgages and it's your tenants' job to pay off your mortgage. This interest only mortgage needs to be paid like a repayment mortgage as a standing order by your tenants as a total rent. This gives you the flexibility to switch back to only paying the interest on the loan if you do run into large un foreseen costs, but do try to avoid this whenever possible, to ensure your portfolio can be self-sustained on repayment mortgages.

Generally, the property market always increases at various rates as the last centuries of history proved, even when the property market temporarily struggles or soar. So if capital appreciation is nearer 2% than 3% yearly, then your current portfolio could be worth £1.3million than £1.6 million. Now imagine if your properties are in London, where many properties almost double yearly, so your current £100,000 portfolio could be £4,000,000 in 20 years time, or £300,000 appreciates to £16,000,000 in 20 years time. This makes an ideal set and forget strategy.

Even if you assume the worst, such as there will be no capital growth over the next 20 years, your tenants has already paid off your mortgage for you and subside the debt. Also, if your budgeted running costs have been less than expected, or your rental income is at its peak and consistent, or you have made an annual profit, then you can either use this profit to pay down existing mortgages or expand this portfolio, or reinvest into a different strategy for short term income. It's entirely up to you. Most successful property investors who adopt this strategy don't take any money out of the portfolio, but also don't put any or very little of their own money into it either. The only optional exception is to contribute to the mortgages with alternative funds to reduce the level of mortgage.

What about my time and tenant management?

Understandably, many landlords aren't enthusiastic when it comes to dealing with the daily management of properties, but this needs to be taken care of, either by letting agents or you encourage your tenants to keep in regular contact via emails or calls or texts. Where repairs are required, you ask them to liaise with a local reliable tradesman who is requested to directly email you quotes and an invoice for the completed repairs.

I will assume you value your time so you may want to limit the number of hours your properties demand, and from experience, a dozen of properties can be achieved with less than 2 hours of input weekly on average. It's really about how effectively you use that time. Occasionally, it could be more than 2 hours if the property is void, or if you are managing a refurbishment, or purchasing another property. If you want hundreds more properties and you lack the time, you can easily find many portfolio builders who overtake all the management, sourcing, legal requirements, protection and financing for you at an agreed fee.

Case study

Jack bought his first investment property that is in a reasonable condition which didn't require refurbishment, therefore only needed to use £15,000 of his money for deposit and legal fees. With the property valuation of £75,000 with an annual 3% increase growing into a £132,000 property after the tenants pay off the 20 years interest only mortgage in a repayment approach. Basically, his £15,000 grows into £132,000 worth of a property mortgage free in 20 years time. When he made more deposit money elsewhere, he became more confident to purchase another 4 properties which he fully refurbished, enabling him to successfully refinance against their higher end valuation. He purchased his sixth property at £52,000 which is a three bedroom terraced house, and spent £9,000 renovating it. The end valuation was £76,000 so he remortgage at 80%, to give him a mortgage balance of £62,000 after the process costs. Basically, by paying down this mortgage over the next 20 years with an assumed 3% annual growth, he could achieve a 6,500% return on his money.

How do you do it?

- You unlock on average an annual 3% increase in the value of your properties, although this depends on where the location is. In prime locations like central London, properties double in value annually.

- You can minimise the management cost by self-managing the properties for an average 2 hours weekly.

- It's more convenience to purchase within 40 minutes drive of where you live, because you can view the properties properly before purchasing, attend the problems promptly, be aware of local new developments affecting your property area, and you would be familiar of its local market and its rental supply/demand.

- Include a calculation on average of 6% interest to be cautious, even though the current rates are much lower.

- Anticipate spending 15% on the annual rent on repairs and maintenance.

- Ensure you only purchase in areas that people will always want to live in, such as the excellent transport links.

- Preferably, the types of properties should be 2 or 3 bedroom houses with a garden which attracts reasonable quality tenants and these types of property are the most common and in demand.

- Each property you purchase should break even at least, but excess income is better for precaution.

1. Purchase price: £75,000
2. Estimated monthly mortgage with average of 6% interest only on a repayment basis: £429
3. Monthly rental income: £500
4. Monthly maintenance/repairs at 10% of rent: £50

5. Estimated end value after 20 years of 3% annual growth: £132,000
6. Estimated monthly rental after 20 years of 3% annual growth: £876

Final note,

You can vary your portfolio by how many properties you prefer, the locations for different growth rate, how much the rent will be, better tenants who pay fully and consistently, the loan to value of the interest only mortgages and more.

Purchase Options and Lease Options

The BTL property investment is now recognisable and increasingly common, normally due to the media, however, what about let-to-buy? A purchase option is a legal agreement, which gives you the control of an asset without actually owning it. An option means the right to buy but not the obligation to do so, at a fixed price and within a certain time period. A purchase lease option is the same as a Purchase Option, with the additional benefit of being able to use the assets in return for a monthly payment which is a rental or lease payment. Therefore you can control a property and receive a rental income from it, without finding the 25% deposit or a mortgage, which is useful if you are unable to raise a mortgage or a large deposit.

Imagine that you are considering buying a property, but you have no money, you have a poor or damaged credit rating and no method of raising deposits, transaction costs or even the loans. With a lease option, you can still buy your property.

An illustration:

You source a property for sale at £100,000. The mortgage on that specific property at 100% would cost roughly £1,000 in monthly mortgage payments. You can afford to pay possibly £900 monthly for it, because you have a regular monthly income but nothing else. To completely expect to be able to get a suitable mortgage, you estimate that it would take you two years to repair your credit. For an easier understanding, you assume that the capital growth on the property is 10% annually.

Imagine approaching the current owner and you suggest the following:

- You suggest at a given date, such as two years in the future, when your credit is repaired, that you agree to purchase the property on a lease option, to gain ownership of the property.
- Before the lease option begins, you agree to pay £900 per month for the two years you live there.
- The future price is agreed by you.

Currently, you and the seller could discuss and agree for any amount. At today's price, such as £100,000, both of you might fix the price at that. This property would be worth £123,000 in two years time, if both of you want to allow for some capital growth, so at 10% per annum capital growth, it's most likely that you both agree an amount amongst these two figures, allow a certain discount for the purchaser and to allow a certain profit for the seller. Now imagine an assumed figure of £110,000 and how this lease option method can be a win-win for both the buyer and the seller.

- You agree that of the £900 you pay monthly, and it will be £230 monthly as a down payment for the deposit on the property in two years time.
- After two years, at roughly over 5% of the agreed purchase price of £110,000 which equates to when you have paid £230 monthly for two years, creating a total of £5,520 as a deposit.
- With your repaired credit you easily get a mortgage for £104,480, as £110,000 minus £5,520, the deposit paid on instalments. This signifies only 86% of the

market value at the time. Therefore, at the end of the two years and when the option matures the property is worth £123,000.

What are the benefits for the seller of the property?

- A guaranteed buyer is available for the seller of the property.
- The seller of the property has a responsible and driven tenant, who is very unlikely to damage it.
- The seller collects £900 per month, paying the mortgage of £500, allowing £230 as a part payment against the future deposit; meanwhile, the seller receives an added £170 monthly without doing anything.
- For £230 monthly to use elsewhere, thus giving the seller a cash flow benefit.
- Although the growth is only 5% annually but it's guaranteed, so the final sales price allows for some profit on the original investment.
- The seller has the further advantage of a bonus £5,520, the deposit which has been collected and which is now forfeited, but only if the purchaser doesn't want the property in two years at the option maturity time, which is the purchasers' option.
- Additionally, the seller can now go and sell their property for £123,500.

What are the benefits for the buyer?

- A place they hope to own and like, the buyer has a guaranteed home to live for two years.
- The buyer can pay the deposit in step payments to the seller in agreement.
- The buyer's credit rating will be sorted out during the two years.
- At the discount of 5% in two years time, the buyer then acquires a property.
- The buyer now has their home in two years time, after starting from a position of having nothing.

Whether you are the buyer or the seller, the process can work for any property transactions. You understand positions where you could take advantage of the arrangement from one side or the other.

- Also by being the middle person, you may really grow experienced enough to handle these options. Imagine that you are the buyer of the property on the quoted terms, using the illustrations above. You may be able to:
- Rent out the property to a third party for two years, such as, at least £1,000 per month, earning your entirely passive £100 monthly income.

In two years time, you may arrange to sell the same property at an agreed price of £57,500. Again, you also receive £5,000 (i.e. £115,000 minus £110,000) for being in the middle, whilst the buyer would still receive a discount to market value.

Understandably, these figures are simple and minimal values, but imagine doing 10 and the margins were larger?

You could build a complete property portfolio income stream using this arrangement, where you just sit there and collect the money, both income on a monthly basis and a lump sum at each option maturity. All you need to do is find the two parties (one seller and one buyer). You never own the properties at all, so this minimises some ownership issues. If you are familiar with day trading, in this case, you could trade the lease options just like options in other commodities.

1. Capital Repayment:

   £130,500 capital spread for the agreed duration in weekly, monthly or quarterly then £20,000 interest lump paid at end.

2. Interest Only Repayment:

   £20,000 interest spread for the agreed duration in weekly, monthly or quarterly then £130,500 capital lump paid at end.

3. Combination Repayment:

   £140,500 interest combined with capital spread for the agreed duration weekly, monthly or quarterly.

Consider how you could arrange a suitable finance arrangement that is win-win for both sides, because there is no 'one size fits all' method. Also some of the examples of who you could use as a money source can be:

- Friends/Family
- Savings from your job
- Equity release
- Angel Investors
- Someone who can enable a pension release
- Overdrafts
- Unsecured and secured Loans
- Credit
- Sourcing agent
- Syndicates
- Property Network members (Recommend)
- Bridging loans
- Builders who normally refurbish with or for property investors
- Many more

BUY TO FLIP

When you are sourcing BMV properties that may be unsuitable to rent out, perhaps the market rents in the area is insufficient to qualify for a BTL mortgage or the area may be unsuitable to let the property out on a multi-let basis. If you afford to purchase it for as little as £40,000 or less, then you could sell it at a higher rate if you have bought the property at a heavy discounted rate, instead of walking away from a quick small profit.

Remember, you may have to pay a CGT on your profit if you are selling any property other than your primary residence. Ideally, the aim for most property investors is to buy more properties than to sell, because you may want the net effect of your overall property portfolio to increase in size. You also have to consider the risk of selling in a static or declining market for property sales, therefore you need to ensure a huge discount of at least 25% BMV to justify flipping it for a decent quick profit. The bigger the discounts, the more profit is left over for you after the purchase costs, holding costs and sale costs is paid when selling at a competitive price to the end consumers. Such as, you purchase a property for £130,000 and it is worth £170,000 then you sell it quickly via the estate agents for a competitive price of £149,950 because it is likely to need refurbishment if it's hugely discounted. Also the potential buyers could be more interested in renting it out long term, instead of the instant equity after refurbishment.

The less time you spend holding the property trying to flip it, the more profit is retained when you are not paying much of the holding costs. Therefore, ensure you choose the right estate agent who is prompt and can market the property with as much exposure to sell your property it quickly. It really helps if you have already established a relationship with an estate agent, because they can work harder for you by aiming at a list of potential investors and buyers looking for this type of property. Also, don't try to negotiate too much on their selling commission as this will discourage them from being motivated enough to sell it quickly for you, therefore you could even suggest a bonus commission if it's sold within a week or sooner.

Compound Growth

The most common and slowest approach is when most people sit on just one property, waiting for it to appreciate in value, such as their own home. However, your own home is a liability that costs you money, because you have to pay expenses on it. In the meantime, and only when you sell it, that it gives a long awaited capital gain, but the supply and demand may change by that time.

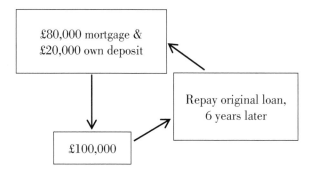

When you have found ways to generate your available amount of money, begin by dividing it into 3 and up to 6 sections. But be careful, as you may not be spreading your risk enough if you have too few, but it might be confusing if you have more than you can handle. Therefore, you need to decide how many sections to be distributed to capital growth with rental income, how many you can gradually handle, and you can hire others to mange them to focus on the big picture.

Then using each sections of money as a deposit, add to it the borrowing you can raise to generate a much larger portion to invest with., and you repay the orginal loan and provide yourself with both the rental incomes generated.

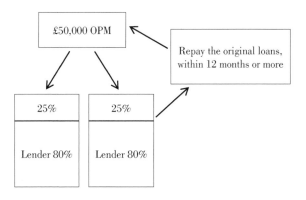

Imagine what you could do with £100,000 loan with this same method, because you could convert £100,000 into a property portfolio worth at least £500,000 as leverage with 5 individual properties. These rental properties could appreciate in value and you can remortgage the whole portfolio, take out more funds and re-invest them to get another group of properties. Eventually the portfolio grows into an expanding collection of properties, although the growth may be slow, depending on the property market. It can be grown quicker if you boost up the appreciation along the way, by borrowing against the following properties. This strategy may be better if done through your company for personal protection, tax benefits and more.

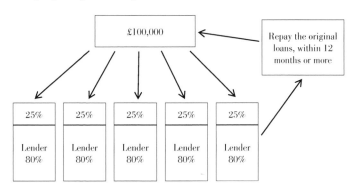

CASH BACK AT COMPLETION

Cash back at completion method exists and happens often, the outcome for this method is to boost your cash flow, so that you may get more money at the beginning, usually when you need it most. Although these deals may be harder to find, it's still worth exploring this option wen you find an opportunity like this. This is usually suitable for people who can quickly rush things to completion, otherwise time cost money.

It would be very beneficial to source a solicitor who will agree to adopt this method with you, although they can be concerned doing all this on the same day, so it's a wise option to offer a day or two between the buy and sell transaction. Generally the quicker the contract is exchanged; then the better it is for everyone. Secondly, a different form of financing is required, because you won't need a 25-year mortgage for this transaction. Consider appropriate short term methods of finances, such as an overdraft or even credit cards or use an alternative fund source.

An illustration:

Cash back at completion is when you may find a property valued at £200,000, but can be purchased at £170,000, therefore may be leftover money at completion. In this situation, as the purchaser you go through all the steps of a gifted deposit method, finds a 90% LTV for the property, you obtain 90% of £200,000 retail market value, which is £180,000 from the lender, but only £170,000 is due to the seller. As a result, there is £10,000 available as cash back on completion day, and you have enough to cover the paperwork costs/fees. This method allows you to create money when you buy the property instead of when you sell. The main way of getting cash back at completion by selling a property successfully whilst buying it is when you do back-to-back property transactions.

1) You source a property that you consider may be undervalued at £100,000, but after some research, you could sell it for £110,000 if the property was advertised properly.

2) After making an offer on the property at £100,000 and the deal begins whilst you exchange contracts for completion.

3) After advertising the property properly at target buyers; a few hours later, you exchange contracts to sell the property for £110,000.

4) You get the £10,000 out at completion as cash from the solicitor.

5) Be aware you have a few necessary fees/legal costs which you prepare in advance, although your costs have been minimal and you made thousands within a couple of hours as a middleperson.

This form of deal is often used when buying off plan, or buying to plan, although you reserve a property on a new development to plan, whilst the buildings are still at plan stage. You confirm your price for purchase with the building development company, and when the property completion date is fixed, you can then search a buyer for 'your' property, clearly at a higher price. It's natural to see prices increase throughout the building stage, and especially if the development is well advertised by the development company, you can often get a significant premium for the property just by being in at the early stages. You can achieve a greater deal if you purchase new development properties, but allocate them on before you become the full owner. In some situations you can even transfer the stamp duty payable onto the new buyer, making the deal even greater for you.

Obviously, you have to fund a deposit at some stage with both these back-to-back approaches. On the other hand, you can agree a small deposit or no deposit if possible, and it's usual for building development companies to fund deposits or refund deposits, or give some other cash as incentives that minimises the cost. Furthermore, you can often secure first position on new developments with a minimal fee of a few hundred pounds before exchanging, which is usually refundable at least, if you don't progress with the purchase.

The quantity you pay as a deposit on any property is simply an arrangement between the seller and the buyer; therefore if you both approve that the deposit should be 5% or even no deposit, it's completely up to both of you. This method is usually more common with private sellers, or those who have control with the deposit arrangements. Furthermore, a deposit can be provided from an insurance policy instead of cash; so you may pay an insurance premium of a few hundreds rather than a deposit of many thousands.

GIFTED OR GHOSTED DEPOSITS

This is another innovative method of purchasing a property at a discount, because there are some people available who want to deal in 'wholesale' prices, and those who want to deal at retail prices. Just like business owners buy clothes at wholesale prices and then as a middle person sell them on at retail prices, so simply think of properties as clothes in the same method. So some people buy properties at wholesale prices and then sell them as retail to the public, therefore buying directly from a property wholesaler. It's a sample of one of many no money down deals, which occurs everywhere and regularly, but it's not a method that everyone is familiar with. It's known as a ghosted deposit arrangement, because you don't use your money for a deposit. You may be familiar with new builds where the developers advertise there is a 10% or 15% deposit paid, which is when they are adopting the exact same method of a ghosted deposit.

An illustration:

Imagine the seller is a selling a property worth £100,000 which is the true retail market value of the property, but he has agreed to sell it to you at a discount at £80,000. In this case, if you can get a mortgage based on the £100,000 retail market value instead of the £80,000 purchase and wholesale price, therefore you can purchase the property without your own money. As a result, you get a mortgage for £80,000 based on 80% of the retail market value of the property, which you pay over to the seller on completion day. Clearly you have not put any money into the deal, if you have purchase the property for £80,000 in finance and the selling price is £80,000, but you are aiming to make a profit. Between the selling price and the market value; you realise your extra 20% difference created. Therefore this method only works if you are buying properties at wholesale prices or below the market value, and the finance provider has to agree with this valuation versus market price type of deal. The loan/mortgage is formed on the open market value of the property instead of the purchase price. Except for the legal and required expenses, this entire transaction can take place with no money being paid by the buyer. This method allows you to create a gain when you sell the property.

You and your team need to be comfortable with this creative strategy, but it's important to be very careful how you adopt this deal. These deals become mortgage fraud IF you artificially inflate the purchase price above the market in order to produce a false value on which to base your mortgage, therefore some advisors and solicitors discourage and warn about this method due to the risk of mortgage fraud. Just ask them to explain what is allowable or not, and ensure you keep everything truthful.

TOOLS TO MAXIMISE WEALTH & MINIMISE RISKS

Mistakes give you wisdom and experience

We all experience mistakes, but we all want success. So why is it that some of us quit as soon as we face challenges, but some of us continue breaking down challenges and come out on top? Or, why is it that some of us settle for ordinary by visualising only the penalties of mistakes, but others willingly fight for their goals by visualising the rewards of success? The most important part about mistakes is learning the lessons from it. Everyone is different, so it's important to understand how you overcome obstacles, and enjoy the journey to your destination of success. Your success can be achieved only by changing your thinking, and not by chance or waiting.

We must all experience mistakes to learn from, either by watching others or by learning from your own, to know the difference between investing the smart way and the average way. Learning from mistakes teaches children and adults to learn useful skills such as hope, determination, experience and resilience which are all essentials to success.

Every successful person you have ever heard of, are always studying and enduring mistakes in all types and proportions along the way, because it's a completely natural part of progressing to success. The main difference is how you can overcome the obstacles, how well you accept that is a natural part of progressing and how much your ambition matters to you. Whilst countless rejections is a natural and expected part of progressing, what matters most, is how you keep getting up and continue in different ways. Therefore, you come out of each obstacle stronger and wiser than before, just like every successful person.

As the great basketball player Michael Jordan once said, "I've missed more than 9,000 shots in my career. I've lost almost 300 games. 26 times I've been trusted to take the game-winning shot and missed. I've failed so many times in my life, and that is why I eventually succeeded."

Understandably, your own journey will include some missed shots and some lost opportunities. Of the hundreds I've questioned and studied regarding property investments, some will completely ignore you, some will charge forward only to give up later, and some will grow into a huge success. Always focus on your goal, but remember the keys to success during the bumpy journey.

– You have to expect temporary mistakes, but giving up makes it permanent and that is the problem. Very often, it's not the obstacles that causes mistakes, it's our expectation of perfection or not trying to overcome it strongly enough. If you understand that property investing will always be full of small changes, and that you fail at some and succeed at others, you are more likely to remain focused and carry on. Even when you feel frustrated or defeated, it doesn't change the situation if you freak out or give up.

– Play the '10 ways' or even '20 ways' game if you can, when the obstacles gets in your way, by listing 10 or more ways you can overcome it. Usually, it could be just the negative talk of others or your own, so you need to brainstorm how to go from inner loser to inner winner.

— Finally, whenever you are faced with difficult situations, it's easy to react negatively, so take a moment to look at the situations from a different perspective. Try to understand what caused the obstacles and what it will take to get the solutions for it. By being open to ideas and possibilities you didn't know existed, you could benefit with some opinions from mentors and experienced property investors, or do some research on how to proceed. Once you are ready, accept and focus on the alternative path you choose.

Overall, as you struggle through the good days and bad days that will surely come in property investing, remember that all the successful people including Michael Jordan, lost a lot of games in order to be the best. Set realistic goals for yourself and your property investments, analyse your successes and mistakes, seek good advice from those supportive of you, whilst remaining focused on your goals. Therefore, if giving up is never an option, then mistakes is simply an opportunity to learn and charge forward. Ensure you do that, and success will surely follow.

Stage 3: Systemised and Exit

The worst thing to do at this stage is to do everything yourself, because if you want to run a multi-million property business, you need a team of people who are effectively managing it all for you, but you still remain in complete control, by working 'on' it, not 'in' it. Whereas, if you try to do everything yourself at this stage, then you are doing more harm than good as you are holding back the business. You need to know how to leverage, utilise systems, outsource and use a supportive team by this stage. To significantly grow your income by turning it into a full-fledged automated business with staffs and paying customers, then understand that you need to let go of your 'baby' and entrust your team and staffs to take the reins. Can you imagine Richard Branson from Virgin currently running his billion dollar enterprise without any staff? You just cannot juggle everything at once.

Imagine if you systematised and packaged your property portfolio into a business, then prepare a mentorship or lending, etc business around this strategies, showing investors how to fully maximise and utilise these strategies with mentorships, and lend out money as a bridging facility, therefore you become an expert in the industry, growing your business, and earn an unlimited income. At this stage, you have a fully automated your business by implementing systems and processes, therefore, you no longer need to deal with low income generating activities, but instead, outsource and leverage them with your team. Would you deny yourself of making more money in terms of liquid cash from educating others, or lending funds, or sourcing deals, etc with your real business?

Avoid being too detailed and getting too stuck in to the small things, otherwise this unnecessary distraction will wither your business to decay, because that is a task for others, while you need to focus on the bigger vision to move the business forward. You don't want to sweat these small stuffs at this stage.

Another vital part that contributes to a successful property investment is building a supportive and great team, who are interdependent on each other for services, or products or information to achieve a team goal. You are a business person and a team leader now, just like Richard Branson and Donald Trump, instead of being the one man band or just a property investor.

Timing and observing trends are another useful skill, because you can certainly predict what will happen, except WHEN it will happen, otherwise we would all be millionaires. Therefore, equipped with your smart education to understand and observe the property market trends, you become the insider with inside knowledge, for clues on when it's potentially the peak times or the dip times to sell or buy. You could buy during the bleak economic times, or when supply is stronger than demand, and then sell slightly before things are in its strongest demand or best economic times. It's always better to be too soon than be too late, because you can't rewind time, but you can fully prepare for the opportunity while you wait. Be the early movers and the early adopters, instead of the late adopters, when looking for the trend movements, and remember a smart property investor can always see plenty of opportunities in any market conditions.

Having an exit plan is a sensible way to protect you from getting hurt. You could let your team manage and grow it continually, or you could sell the business, convert it into a shareholding company as an IPO, or let it go static.

If you are considering growing your business, then it will have plenty of space to grow within the early stages, but understandably, it could be a wobbly process during a bleak economic time. Be flexible by cushioning yourself for those wobbly times, by using your smart knowledge and strategies converting the disadvantages into your advantages. You could have the option to sell at peak prices when strong buyer demands arise for properties, whilst it's currently rented in a strong rental demand market. Also, a bleak economic time allows you to purchase properties at heavily discounted prices, while private lenders increase, becoming more creative and flexible than conventional mortgage providers. Make your business as recession-proof as possible and the peak times will take care of itself.

Alternatively, acquisition is the most usual exit for an entrepreneur or business owner, therefore if you are considering selling your business, and then begin the process by ensuring the system documents are updated about the management of the business for potential buyers. However, if you can sustain the income steady at this stage without any dips, you will be doing really well, while you are focused on the selling preparation.

- Understand from the buyer's perspective, such as their motivations and expectations, as they may be more interested in potential for stable revenue streams and growth potential, whereas you are more interested in creative strategies and innovation. A buyer's motivation can differ to the typical business owner's.

- Don't let the business's success be too dependent on you, by training your management team to take over the critical business functions, because the buyer wants to buy your business instead of you or your job. Otherwise, if all the key decisions depend on you, then this limits the value of the business and the buy will feel discouraged.

- Continue managing and growing your business, because you want to avoid getting too wrapped up in either the sales process or entirely in a sale offer, therefore ensure you monitor your business's operations with a laser sharp focus. It's very practical to act as if any deal can fall through, even if you are in the final negotiation period, because any deal can come undone at the last minute, therefore continue managing and growing your business until the funds have cleared and in the bank.

- Ensure you keep the sales process confidential, because you want to avoid the risks of any key clients, employees, and team members or partners departures endangering the transaction or the operations of your business.

- Don't wait too long to sell, avoid being like many business owners who wait until the last minute to try and sell their business. Your business could stagnates while you wait too long, or when you become exhausted with the management of the business, therefore the best time is when the business is booming.

- Don't be in too much of a hurry, otherwise you will likely leave a lot of money on the table, because buyers such as sophisticated larger corporations may sense your urgency, and take advantages of it during the negotiation period.

- Start the process early, by preparing 2 to 4 years before the sale with consistently recorded and compiled records over a few years. Otherwise it's much more costly and time-consuming to rush and prepare all the necessary financial and relevant information in a few months. This record-keeping is also important for your business's growth, since it provides more perspective on your company's performance.

- Get your business in order, by ensuring you have kept accurate financial records and prepared all your assets for sale, such as tangible and intangible assets, ensure that everything is transferable to the potential buyer and expect an extensive due diligence.

Recognising an ideal area to invest in

Finding a 100% perfect location to invest in is very rare, but you can easily identify what defines a suitable area to invest in. The ideal location could be anywhere, providing you can find a stable supply of tenants with a strong demand, and where the numbers makes financial sense for you. But all areas and economic climates can change, and what was a desirable area last year, may not be now, due to many things like changes in rent, sale prices, and local supply and demand. The same applies to what may not be a desirable area now, could become the opposite in the future. Whilst there is no such thing as a good or bad area to invest in, although the crucial point is in sourcing a property where there are suitable tenants in supply, and where the rent you need to reach your required return is promising. Ultimately, all you need is one responsible tenant to make your investment work for you.

Assess the property and the location as an outsider instead of as a homeowner. Consider these properties as an investment commodity instead of somewhere you imagine you plan to live in, so decorate the property in a neutral and impersonal décor. Purchase properties that minimises hassle, which means managing and maintaining them easily or getting it managed for you. Continually review the property and your strategy, and don't just forget about it, as things change and you might find that investment suddenly or gradually miss your minimum targets. The crucial point is to watch an area for a while, each time do your homework and check what type of properties there are, how much they cost and if they rent easily or not. You can find all this information from the local agents, local newspapers, on the internet or just ask around locally.

You have a list of 15 suggestions that gives a vague idea of how to recognise a suitable area to invest in, when buying an investment property. Remember to define yourself some minimum requirements before searching for a location. Importantly, be realistic as no area is 100% perfect, otherwise you will wait a long time to find that. Carry a clipboard of checklists if visiting or searching information on an area when deciding a location to invest in.

1. Up and coming

You can get into an up and coming location early, as soon as the government decides to push up property prices by creating employment, building a hospital, or a university, as this will all cause a ripple effect on surrounding lower priced areas. Check out for any news on government intervention, regional development, development such as educational and leisure, and grant or housing employment subsidy, which are causes of ripple effect. Therefore, people who want to live in the upmarket area, but are unable to afford it, so they move to the up and coming area as the next best thing. Property prices ripple outwards, so buy before it increases in value.

2. Maximum ease

Properties that require consents of any kind or are listed can be more problematic, because you can't maintain or improve the property as you prefer. Any alteration or refurbishment has to be made in agreement with the criteria of that grading for listed properties. If you decide to purchase a property of this type, then ensure that you completely understand the requirements of the listing or the consents required for any works. Meanwhile, these expensive and difficult processes won't give you much ease, and the same can be true for structurally damaged properties that require hiring structural engineer or builders.

3. Capital growth potential

The simplest route for this is to buy properties which are well cared for, but its potential is undeveloped, such as a loft conversion, adding a conservatory, updating the bathroom and kitchen. While you are renting the property out, you could even arrange a planning permission to convert the property into flats as HMO if allowable. The property needs to be well cared to enable to continue getting tenants easily, but the possibilities exist to develop the property when you have more money and time in the future. Having this bonus maximises your financial opportunity from a property.

4. Secure and safe property

Safety is important in not just the location alone; therefore, a property with tough external doors, security alarm, window locks and fenced garden will be advantageous and makes the potential tenants feel safer.

5. Clean and open surroundings

People normally feel happier if they have hygienic and bright spaces around them, therefore, select properties where the streets are well lit, reasonably quiet and wide, and preferable, some open space such as a park or greenery nearby. Even if the property may be cheaper because it's situated in an undesirable location, you may be limiting potential tenants and buyers as a result and check out its crime rate on websites such as www.upmystreet.com

6.   Minimum requirements for space

You could ensure that the main bedroom fulfils a minimum size to fit in a double bed with ample space for storages, and you may do the same for other rooms. If possible, properties with high ceilings are even better, as this makes the rooms appear bigger; similarly, neutral colours, clever mirroring and lightings will give a bigger impression of space.

7.   Having a garage or off street parking

This is particularly important for professional people who work full time as they want speed and convenience of their own parking arrangements. Also, because they are at work all day with nobody at home, they need to feel their car is safe if they leave it at the property. If a property is situated directly to a school, then off street parking at certain times may be tricky, unless a garage of their own is available.

8.   Having a external access if it's a flat

This is important for people to feel that there is a way out of their property, because it makes them feel safe. Therefore it's vital for people not to feel trapped in a property, and having just a small outdoor space or patio at least makes them feel that they can go outside and sit if preferable.

9.   Practical layouts

Having a practical layout allows the property to be lived in by a large amount and mixture of people. If you want to have families as your tenants, then ensure that the bedrooms are together and that the bathroom is conveniently placed, so the children can sleep near their parents and access the bathroom easily. Open plans are very popular for its practicality. However, if a couple move in without children, there is no hindrance to the position of the bathrooms or bedrooms. You would still own a property with its practical layout which can fit a family or a couple when you prefer to let to that type.

10. Supplying a first time buyer demand

A first time buyer market always exist, but this demand varies depending on the supplies and other effects. Those who need to rent a property for the first time, such as a one bedroom flat or studio, are people who are leaving home for the first time, or people who are getting married or divorced may want just a simple 2 bedroom property. All these types of people need somewhere to live, and this type of property is suitable at some stage in their lives, regardless of the overall property market. Therefore, to benefit from this varying demand, ensure you can provide a few or more properties that are suitable for first time buyers.

11. Good local facilities

It's very beneficial to have a property that is reasonably close to good local facilities such as shops, a pub, roads and bus stops, because very few people want to be completely isolated, so enable them to do their shopping, get to work and have a social life. You might decide a set limit of 5 or 10 minutes walk to these facilities, which could assist in your property searches or when instructing the sourcing agents.

12. Good local transport links

Your potential tenants may prefer easy and convenience access to employment and other facilities, and it's useful if there are transport choices such as bus, trams and a train station, which maximises the chances of attracting tenants. But if the property is too exposed and situated next to a very busy major road, a family will feel it's too risky with the children.

13. A separate toilet from the bathroom

This is for flexibility and convenience and will create that added bonus when potential tenants are viewing your property. This simple thing could be one of the major reasons in preference to yours to another, therefore, it could make the difference between you getting tenants and having void periods.

14. Minimal noise and smell

None of us really want to live next door to the neighbours from hell or at the end of the runway of Heathrow, therefore a property situated next to a major noisy road or a roaring airport, could be very noisy unless the windows can silence the noise. Be careful when selecting properties that are very near major sources of noise and smell such as near the pubs, and night clubs. Being too directly close to retail food outlets such as a flat above a chip shop always has a smell and the food rubbish could attract unwanted pests and rodents.

15. Environmentally and ecologically safe

It's advisable to purchase a property that is high above the flood plains without risks to any flooding, because nobody wants to be flooded, it would be tricky for you as a landlord to sort out, and you struggle to get adequate insurance. Check with the local council for areas at potential risk, because families with young children may refuse to live close to landfill sites, radon, masts, incinerators and pylons, therefore, avoid anything that may cause problems later or may restrict your potential returns.

SQUEEZING THE RETURNS

The 'squeezing the return' method is to regularly squeeze more of the returns from the portfolio, by analysing the lowest performing one. If you can improve the return, then do it, but if you can't, then consider replacing the property for an alternative with higher performing return. Therefore, by regularly reviewing the portfolio in this way, you can squeeze more of the returns on the portfolio. Obviously, it's easy to see why mature and strong portfolios normally have higher returns, than new and partly invested portfolios, due to the advantage of the return squeezing process over time.

Imagine that you are calculating returns using the cash on cash return basis of calculation, perhaps you may have 5 properties and their returns are 30%, 21%, 10% and 25% on average.

You analyse the lowest return property to see if you can improve it, or drive it up, or in this case, it's the lowest one producing 10% return.

Imagine that the figures look like this:

+ Gross Rent £1,000
— Mortgage £600
— Management fee £100
— Other costs £100
+ Net cash monthly £200

Calculation: £200 x 12 months = annual return of £2,400

Your original input was, perhaps, £16,000 as the deposit on £106,000 and your net return is £2,400 annually and as a percentage of £16,000 at 15%. (£2,400 / £16,000 x 100 = 15%)

To squeeze more of the return you need to challenge the entire financials on that individual property, by asking questions like:

> Could you decrease the management fee?
> Could you improve the mortgage/loan deal or get a better one elsewhere?
> Could you decrease some of the expenses, by checking around for more competitive deals on the insurance and maintenance, etc?
> Could you increase the rent a little?
> If you can't squeeze enough return, then can you afford a better property deal elsewhere?

If you can improve the return by taking some, or all, of these actions, you now recalculate the return, and imagine you recognise that the cash on cash return on your money is now 30% as follows:

- \+ Gross Rent £1,100
- — Mortgage £550
- — Management fee £80
- — Other costs £70
- \+ Net cash monthly £400

Calculation: £400 x 12 months= annual return of £4,800, which is a percentage of £16,000 at 30%.

When the portfolio is mature and stronger with improved returns than the ones you currently have, you can gradually strengthen the wealth of your property portfolio with higher returns than ever. As a result, you now have the experience and the bonus of selecting only the best investment properties. Therefore, you see that this property is not the lowest performer now, so, it remains in the portfolio and you begin assessing the next lowest, such as the 21% and so on.

Recognising a positive cash flow investment

Property Analysis

- Retail Market value: £129,000
- Discounted at 30% BMV: £89,950
- Instant Net Equity on Completion £39,050
- Fees and cost total: £4,795

Property features:

- Development potential to be unlocked, therefore a total refurbishment is required. Similar properties in finished condition in same location are compared as £129,000 at Retail Market Value.
- Freehold type.
- Semi-detached with 3 bedrooms and 1 bathroom situated in a town.

Area features:

Country walks
Golf

Motorway link
Pubs
Restaurants
Schools
Shops
Supermarket
Town centre within 5 miles
Train station

Financial breakdowns:

- Market rent: £700 per calendar month
- Retail Refurbished Valuation: £129,000
- Purchase price: £89,950
- Yield on ROI: 9%
- Vendor legal fees: £700
- Sourcing fee: £1,995
- Marketing fee: £2,000
- Reservation online fee: £100
- Refurbishment cost: Estimated £25,000
- Equity on Completion: £39,050 with deal fees of £4,795 excluding VAT, Stamp Duty and legal disbursements.

Obviously, each property deals will vary in all the costs shown above, and it can be influenced by the company who sources them, the market condition, the strength of the demand/supply for the property, your strategy and negotiation strength and more. The main insurance which is legally required is the property, but the optional insurances can be for contents, legal costs of eviction, damage by tenants and void periods. The higher the risk, the more the insurances will charge you.

Below is a few of the many useful contacts available to help ease your journey as a landlord.

Remember, if you are considering a mortgage:

1. Work out how much the mortgage is going to cost you.
2. Multiply the monthly interest by 125% to give the required rent.
3. Check the actual rent is more than the required rent, otherwise move onto the next property.

ANALYSING THE POTENTIAL INVESTMENT

Net equity calculation

1. Calculate the net monthly gain after expenses for the property. This net monthly gain will be the rent money received minus any mortgage payments, taxes, insurance or regular maintenance. For example, you earn £2,000 per month in rent. You pay £1,000 for the mortgage payment—including taxes and insurance—and then spend approximately £300 per month on repairs. Your net monthly gain is £700.

2. Determine the current equity owned on the home. Equity is figured by referencing a mortgage statement, or calling the bank to find a pay-off amount. Take the pay-off amount and subtract it from the current market value, or the tax assessed value of the home, which you can find on your latest tax statement. Subtract these two numbers to find out how much equity you have in the home.

3. For example, you owe £100,000 on a £250,000 home. The current market value for your home is £265,000 according to your latest tax assessment. This means that you have £165,000 in equity in your home after you subtract £100,000 owed minus the assessed value of £265,000.

4. Multiply the net monthly gain by 12 and divide that value by the equity owned on the home. For example, in Step 1 you have a £700 monthly gain. Multiply this

by 12 months which gives you £8,400 in net income per year. Divide £8,400 by £100,000 in equity and that leaves you with 0.084. Multiply the resulting value by 100 to receive a percentage value of the return on investment. After multiplying, your return on investment percentage is 8.4 yearly. That means every year that you own the home, you are earning 8.4% in returns on your money.

5. It's vital to recalculate this value over time to see how the return on investment changes as the equity on the home, net monthly gain and value of the home will change.

Net yield Calculation

1. Calculate how much you would earn from the real estate. Add up the money you would bring in from renting out or leasing the property each month. Do not deduct any expenses yet. Multiply the number by 12 to get the yearly total.

2. Add up your expenses for the real estate. Include taxes, insurance, mortgage payments and repairs and any other expenses pertaining to the property. Be sure to convert all numbers to yearly numbers. For example, you may have expenses of £1,500 a year for taxes, £50 a month (£600 a year) for insurance, £375 a month (£4,500 a year) for mortgage payments and £400 a year for repairs. That would be a total of £7,000 a year for expenses.

3. Figure the amount you have invested. Down payments and costs of repairs made before renting or leasing the property are considered investments. Repairs made while you are renting or leasing the real estate fall under expenses. For example, if you put £15,000 down on the real estate and made £5,000 in initial repairs then your total investment is £20,000.

4. Compute the net operating income. Your net operating income, or NOI, can be found by taking the total amount that you would earn from renting or leasing the real estate and subtracting the total expenses. That number will be your NOI. If your yearly earnings were £8,400, your NOI would be £8,400-£7,000 = £1,400. So, £1,400 would be the net on ROI.

5. Use the NOI to get the ROI. Divide the NOI by your total investment amount. The number that you will get will need to be converted to a percentage by moving the decimal point two places to the right. Using the example below, the ROI would be £1,400/£20,000 = 0.07, which would be 7% for the ROI.

Net Yield Calculation

Annual Rent (1)	£10,000
Annual Operational Costs (2)	£1,000
Property Value (3)	£100,000
Net Yield %	9%
(1)-(2) / (3) x 100 = 9%	

Net Equity Calculation

Annual Gross Rent (1)	£10,000
Annual Operational Costs (2)	£1,000
Total Financed cost (3)	£8,000
Annual Net Rent (4)	£9.000
Equity ROI %	112%
(4) / (3) x 100 = 112.5%	

The purpose of your asset

With passive investments, you avoid the headaches and time associated with active real estate investing, whilst receiving a monthly rental income, because the property management is taken care of. This frees up your time, which is why it is called passive income. Passive real estate investing also allows you more opportunity to diversify their investment portfolio and spread the risk. You don't go to work each day to earn passive income, although managing your investments may still require minimal work to ensure everything is progressing well as expected. The more and bigger the passive incomes, the closer to financial and personal freedom you achieve.

Capital Growth vs. Rental Return

When discussing property investment there are two somewhat conflicting philosophies of property investment. Some suggest you should invest in property for high rental return while others feel you should invest for capital growth (the increase in value of the property.)

We would all like to buy properties that have both great capital growth and a high rental yield, and this is possible when you recognise what the right location and the right property at the right time is to enable to do this.

In regional centres and many secondary locations you can generally achieve a higher rental returns but may generate poor long term capital growth. However in the major capital cities of the UK strong capital growth usually goes with a lower rental yield (the income earned over a year represented as a percentage of the value of the property.)

As the value of a property increases, then it follows that the rental returns may decrease. This is of course unless the rent increases by the same proportion, which does not normally happen. Rents eventually go up but these increases lag capital increases by a number of years.

So the situation during any extended period of high capital growth as happens during property booms is that rental returns fall, because the supply and demand has flipped the to opposite.

And now in the slower phases of the property cycle, when interest rates are rising and affordability of properties are decreasing, more potential home owners are turning to renting properties. This is the stage of the property cycle that rental growth starts to catch up, as is clearly happening in all our capital cities at present.

I understand why most investors would prefer a higher yield. They feel they need the higher rental returns to pay their mortgage. They also believe they cannot buy many properties because they can't afford to service additional loans.

I guess that is why many new investors make the mistake of viewing their property investments as income driven. Yet I still believe that is strong capital growth that will be the key to a successful property investment. Even though the first year or two of holding an investment property can be challenging, but capital growth may build your equity much faster than loan re-payments and rental income will.

So I suggest you seek a balance between growth and income and view your investment as medium to long-term and be prepared to ride out the cycles. The rental income needs to be strong enough to help with your holding costs such as loan repayments, insurance and rates. But it should not be the main reason for investing, unless you are retired and are just looking for income to maintain your lifestyle.

High (Passive Efficiency)

Gazelle:	Lion:
High Efficiency and Low Growth	**High Efficiency and High Growth**
When property prices fall due to low demand in sales, but rental prices grow due to high rental demand.	When property prices grow due to high demand in sales, and rental prices grow due to high rental demand. Such as the most desirable and expensive areas.
Tortoise:	Elephant:
Low Growth and Low Efficiency	**Strong Growth and Low Efficiency**
When property prices fall due to low demand in sales, and rental prices fall due to low rental demand, which is rare due to the law of supply and demand.	When property prices grow due to high demand in sales, but rental prices fall due to low demand.

Low   (Growth Potential)   High

Team Support

Building a great and supportive team has many advantages, such as helping your business to grow, minimises total dependency on you, stronger motivation to succeed, offers you the capabilities that you may lack and many more. Although building a team can be a challenging process itself, it has a worthy purpose, because this helps to put your business on the map, the daily management will be taken on by your team members, your role will be taking board meetings, inspiring and leading the team into new directions, and helping to grow your brand vision.

However, it's important to know the huge differences between a team and a group, because you can't have the same expectations of a group as with a team, therefore recognise which one you are working with. A team shares a leadership and is interdependent on each other for information, services and tasks to achieve a team goal. Like Apple and Steve Jobs, being the leadership is mostly about inspiring people and your team, when they can believe and buy into that, then your business will grow very fast. Whereas a group or employees merely work alone most of the time with minimal dependency, therefore it's a group effort without being supportive of each other.

At Stage 3 of 'Systemised and exit', you understand that your role is very different, because you keep team members responsible and on the same path, by spending more time leading and less time doing, because this would give your business recognition, discover new ways to grow it and you could even franchise the business.

Imagine; if you want to uphold a growth rate of 30% on your business, you need the help of your team to achieve your desired goals, by delegating the control to the relevant members, instead of overwhelming yourself by being the one man team. You have to let go of your 'baby' for it to grow and exceed your goals, or it will always be a baby and just a paid hobby, even if it's difficult for you when you have always done it 'your way'.

It helps if the team have complimentary skill sets, where you are the visionary and move the brand forward, while others are focused on the operations, the details, the analytics and spread-sheets. You could be a technician and a visionary altogether, but be prepared to necessarily adapt your mind to survive if required.

Set up your office:	Building your team:
Laptop	Finance brokers
Real Estate software, contracts, forms	Tax professional
Fax machine & printer	Sourcing Agents or Sourcing Websites
Work phone	Letting or Real Estate Agents
Voicemail/answering machine	Mentor/Coach
Area map	Contractors
Camera	Real Estate lawyer
Recording files for important documents	Insurance agent
Calendar	Property Valuer/Inspector
General office supplies	Banker
Database of all useful contacts	Solicitor (Familiarised with property investment processes)

Referral contacts	Name	Business address	Contact numbers & Email	Company website
Finance Broker A				
Tax accountant				
Finance source				
Builders				
Tax Advisor				
Solicitor				
Mentor				
Wealth Management				
Sourcing agent				
Structural surveyor				
Other				

Networking & Mentors

You could gain invaluable insight beyond your own education and experience when you network with others who are investing or invested in what you plan to do and you could give yourself the edge with the support and guidance of a mentor. Whether you need advice or a sounding board, a mentor can inspire and guide you. Most mentoring programs are designed primarily for the benefit of you and you are encouraged to begin the relationship with specific goals and expectations-which are typically met by a well designed program. Your benefits may extend far beyond what you planned, more than what this book could offer and may include:

What Mentoring and attending network meetings offer you	Your involvement duties
Access to a support system during critical stages of your beginning and progressing development	Be responsible for your career goals and would enjoy the benefit of a mentor's guidance to create a plan for success.
An insider's perspective on navigating your property business	Be ready to listen, but also ready to share your ideas so it's a give and take relationship.
Clearer understanding and enhancement of practical and possible plans	Be ready for objective feedback to consider new ideas and new approaches suggested by your mentor.

Exposure to diverse perspectives and experiences	You have realistic expectations for my mentor relationship. No one is perfect and good relationships take honesty, effort and time.
Direct access to powerful resources within your property business	You may be busy with family and work, but you are ready to make a commitment for your future by communicating with your mentor.
Identification of possibilities gaps	Understand that you only work smarter, not harder
Greater knowledge of property investment success subjects	Willing to think like a successful multi-millionaire, by challenging your original perspective
The foundation of a lasting professional network	To eventually work ON the investment business, instead of IN it, by using other people's time, money and labour

Search and list all the relevant property investment networks available, some can only be attended once a month, while others are more often. Also webinars are growing in popularity for the time conscious investors, but I would recommend attending some networks, to ask questions, demonstrate some ideas or possibilities on paper, meet a mentor who are normally happy to help you on a regular basis for free or at a small charge. You can discuss with other students and experienced property investors about their experiences, and how some overcame the same situation you are in, or to find answers for any of your relevant questions and obstacles.

Organise some information before meeting a possible mentor who will assess your current situation and your expectations, by fulfilling the following:

- Display a professional assessment of your finances, goals and experience level.
- List the types of strategies you be interested in and why you think it will benefit you the most
- Show some examples of actual properties you have searched that you invest in and what its ROI is.
- A thorough evaluation of the property market in your preferred investment area.
- List all the possible sources of finance you are aware of, but mentors and network members can recommend more varieties that you didn't know existed.

LEGAL LETTING CHECKLIST

1. Choose the right location and property:

Always research the target area and the property thoroughly before choosing to invest, because the local amenities, transport links, schools, etc, will all have an effect on the value and rental demand for your property. Ensure you consult local letting agents and check online to determine the supply and demand for rental properties in the area you are considering investing and find out the average rental yield of similar properties on the street. Research recent comparable sales and rental achievements, and beware of discounts being offered by developers looking to offload new developments. Any discount offering is put to you by a company looking to benefit from you, therefore may be ignored by lenders in the current market. Off-plan buying has its place and it's time, but you need to check if it's financially suitable for you.

2. Define the tenant profile:

Think about who your tenant is likely to be, such as professional, family, student, etc and present the property to their needs and expectations accordingly. Don't produce a five star property where the local rental market only requires student accommodation. Also, mod cons such as Wi-Fi can help secure the right tenant. If the property is classed as an HMO (House in Multiple Occupation), ensure the property has a licence to operate from the local council, otherwise you not be able to secure finance on the property without it.

3. Talk to a specialised broker:

Some buy-to-let mortgages are not directly available, so to get a complete picture of the finance available, consider using an independent specialist broker, which has access to the whole of the target type of mortgage such as BTL only. They will have the experience needed to match your borrowing requirements with the most suitable products available. Also, their business volumes and longstanding relationships with lenders often afford their clients preferential processing treatment on mortgage applications. Buy-to-let mortgages are not regulated, so ensure you use a broker that is a member of the National Association of Commercial Finance Brokers. Also don't rely on house prices to rise rapidly.

4. Monitor buy-to-let rates:

Don't just get a BTL mortgage and forget about it, because you can get better deals by monitoring market rates and compare them to your BTL mortgage. Check to see if switching to another rate makes more financial sense, but remember, buy a property to let is a business. Therefore, you owe it to your business to ensure you are getting the best deal possible.

5. Maintain your investment property:

How your property looks can mean the difference between tenants renewing or signing that first lease, therefore weigh up the pros and cons of managing the property yourself or pay a letting agent to manage it. A letting agent will find the right tenant, collect the deposit with the rent and arrange the inventory and tenancy agreements. However, they don't come cheap, so expect to be charged anything from 10% to 17.5% of the gross rental income you receive. A cheaper alterative might be to take out a maintenance contract with an emergency repair firm.

6. Check your tenant:

It's important to undertake credit reference checks on new tenants and tenant referencing checks can cost less than £10 per person. You could also ask for an employer's reference. An **undesirable tenant** probably has poor rental or financial histories that can be uncovered with a thorough check. You should review previous landlord relations, credit reports, court records and income. A passport or driving licence should be cross-referenced with the tenants' application. Ensure that there are no faults and inconsistency within the application, because careful due diligence can save you a lot of expense and emotional stress. Simply search for Tenant referencing companies online for plenty of options.

7. Get a professionally prepared lease:

You could forfeit many of the legal rights afforded to you without a professionally prepared lease, as most basic leases do not take account of your preferences.

8. Protect the tenant's deposit:

If you take a deposit from a tenant on an assured short-hold tenancy agreement, the law in England and Wales states you must protect it with a government-authorised tenancy deposit protection scheme within 14 days. Otherwise, failure to protect the deposit could result in you having to compensate the tenant with up to three times the amount of the deposit, and you may not be able to regain possession of the property. You need to give the tenants details of where it is protected in a scheme, either in a custodial scheme such as www. depositprotection.com or an insurance-based scheme like www.mydeposits.co.uk or www.thedisputeservice.co.uk Also, collect the first month's rent before the tenancy starts and you have established a standing order via their bank.

9.   Get landlord insurance:

You are responsible for insuring the structure of the property, which includes any permanent fixtures and fittings. Also, it's vital to get the right cover, because many building insurance policies exclude buy-to-let. Landlord insurance is designed specifically for rental properties and covers circumstances not covered by normal household insurance. In addition to the usual perils that are covered by standard buildings and contents policies, specialist cover for buy-to-let properties includes protection from the sort of damage or losses that can arise, if you end up with problem tenants. If you own multiple properties, you could save money using an insurer that will provide cover for all properties on a single policy. Ensure that the tenancy agreement has been properly signed, and witnessed if necessary, and that you both have copies. If you need a guarantor signatory, like from a parent, ensure you have this before allowing the tenant in your property.

10. Confirm everything is checked:

Also check the inventory with the tenant, and ensure you both have signed the inventory checklist. Ensure the gas safety check has been checked and both you and the tenant have copies of this report. Explain and show the tenant how everything in the property functions, and leave them copies of the instruction manuals for all the appliances. Read all the meters with them and ensure you have changed all utility bills and telephone bills into their name. Ensure that the tenant knows what to do in an emergency and knows how to contact you if necessary. It's vital to have a spare set of keys when giving the original keys to your new tenant and give sufficient notice to them when you will inspect the property periodically.

11. Keep accurate records:

It is important to keep accurate records of each rental property you own, because you have to pay income tax on any rental income you receive, although you can deduct some expenses. You also probably be liable for Capital Gains Tax (CGT) when you sell. Therefore, it's wise to consult an accountant before you enter the market. A simple spread sheet will do, but if you have lots of properties, it might be worth using specialist software or employing the services of a bookkeeper. So don't lose out on tax breaks by being careless on your paperwork.

12. Rent collections:

The scenario of allowing the tenant to move in before funds have cleared will cause unnecessary headaches for you having to initiate eviction procedures if you have never collected deposit, because you didn't wait for the funds to clear first. Always request money orders, certified cheques or simply wait for the funds to clear your bank before allowing access and occupation. If a tenant fails to pay you rent for 2-weeks and legal notices are not served, you would have allowed a potentially costly pattern. You should never accept partial payments as the courts interpret this as an acceptance of terms by you. If a tenant persists in late rental payments, you should consider not renewing the lease or issuing a notice to quit, because poor payment habits can lead a route to tenant bankruptcy and costly eviction.

13. Get accredited:

It can be a lonely business managing rental property, but you can get support from your local council, many of which offer accreditation schemes to help landlords operate successfully, legally and safe-guard tenants' interests. You can consider joining a trade body or landlord association and discuss useful tips at your local Property networks. To get a perspective of the costly damage of being unaware of what you are doing as an investor/landlord, imagine trying to play a league sport without knowing the rules of the game. So, don't wait until the last minute to develop a professional relationship with a specialist property solicitor, because the necessity of an immediate response to an adverse situation could be very costly.

14. Monitor costs and income:

Calculate and check exactly how much your monthly mortgage repayments will be, and whether the expected rental income will comfortably exceed this. Along with the letting agent's fee, consider the cost of maintaining the property and look at how long you would be able to pay the mortgage if the property gets unoccupied. Could you afford to decrease the rent to get tenants in? You may be paying a letting agent a monthly fee to manage the property, furthermore, paying service charges and ground rent if there is a lease. You are also responsible for ensuring the property complies with health and safety standards.

15. Keep a professional landlord/tenant relationship:

You must always maintain the highest professional relationship with the tenants, to avoid the pitfall of not employing the codes of conduct that are based on the conditions of the lease. Over informality can change the nature of the business relationship, and threaten your ability to collect rents.

16. Ensure good customer service:

Running a BTL portfolio requires the same commitment as running any other business. Good customer service certainly contributes to continuous success. Remember that you would not be in business if it were not for your tenants. Overall, a positive approach to communicating with your tenants will be reflected in the profitability and value of a property. Also, the leading reason tenants do not renew their leases is due to poor response and execution for service requests from the landlords, therefore maintenance requests linked to a diary reduces stress and costs, too.

17. Flexibility on rent

Appallingly low numbers of house sales in the current property market has left vendors taking huge hits on the price in order to shift their home—and unfortunately things are no different for landlords. So although you may be reluctant to drop to £500 a month in rent from your planned £700, if the dispute results in the property standing empty for a month that is £500 down the drain anyway. What's more, being flexible will mean you fall into favour with your tenants from the outset which can only be a good thing.

Using a Letting Agent or not

At the outset there are a variety of different letting and managing agents who have different specialisms, some for example only deal with students and many don't deal with students at all. And of course, they all charge different rates and you can negotiate a special rate for you. Obviously, the more properties you have, the more negotiating power you have with potential agents. This can often be trial and error and you may need to speak to many agents, before you find the right one for you, but clearly if you can get a personal recommendation from someone you know and trust, then that will help.

Deciding to use a letting agent or not depends on the property, the location of that property, the type of person you are and the amount of time you have. So there is no one definitive answer here, so you need to look at the different options.

Firstly, the agent sources, inspects each tenant for you, and get the appropriate references. They will advertise the property, process applications, arrange the tenancy agreement, check the references, and move the tenant in. Secondly, the agent covers the first step and collects the monthly rent as specified and they will deduct their fee and then forward the balance to you regularly.

Thirdly, the managing agent should do everything, including the first two steps and, also they control the tenancy and handle daily queries, problems and maintenance. They will normally discuss the criteria for management with you, such as, asking them to deal with all repairs of up to £100 in cost if preferable, or asking them to handle all repairs, or none, or whatever you prefer. With this full management service you will never be involved with the property at all, and the agent will move tenants in and out, while maximising the period of tenancy, ensuring that you have minimal void periods. This service will also comprise inventory checks and periodic checks on the property, ensuring all is fine.

The costs of agents differ immensely, but as a guide, they perhaps start at about 7% and even increases to 15%. Clearly, the fee increases with the more you ask them to fulfil, but you need to create a strong relationship with any agent that you use, and hopefully you get a better arrangement if you use the agent for a long time or for many properties.

Although, not all agencies offer every form of service and some purposely only provide tenant searches, or some don't deal with students, HMO, DSS tenants or as specified. So you need to find any agencies that can accept your planned strategy, which suits you and your property.

If you want to manage the property yourself, you need to basically cover the following:

1. Advertise your property with as much exposure to attract many potential tenants.
2. Deal with all the enquiries from the potential tenants.
3. Organise viewings of the property.
4. Arrange a system for safeguarding the correct information and appropriate references, preferably you need these from their previous landlord, a bank, credit report, employers, and possibly also a character

reference as well. The more you can obtain, the more confident you feel about the tenant being reliable.

5. Choose the most suitable tenant for you.
6. Organise and approve the tenancy contract and also the inventory list.
7. Check the tenant into the property.
8. Handle any maintenance issues or problems during the tenancy.
9. When the tenant decides to move out, resolve all outstanding concerns and repay the protected deposit.

DEFINING YOUR POTENTIAL TENANTS

1. <u>Families</u>

The property needs to be easily maintained and have a garden and garage. It would be near the local schools, the park, the local swings and the swimming pool. The house would be in a more private area of town or city, where there is minimal traffic, as the children need to be kept safe constantly. You need to offer safe and comfortable accommodation with children in mind for families. It's possible that the property will have at least three bedrooms, and it's possible that the family is in transition between homes, or maybe re-locating due to employment.

2. <u>Couples</u>

It's likely that tenants in this type are planning to save up to purchase their own home, perhaps the sharers will be hoping to acquire their own property, so it's possible that the length of tenancy contracts will be shorter than for singles. Generally, you can group couples and two people sharing into the same general categories as singles. Though, the difference is that surely for sharers, the property requires two bedrooms, so it may needs to be larger.

3. <u>Singles</u>

Even within this type you have a diversity of other options, although these three classifications are 'loosely brushed' and simplistic, it would provide some general guidelines to know about.

Do you want to attract manual or blue-collars or up-market professionals, or semi professional office workers? In each situation, the property differs in appearances and is in a different location. So for the blue-collar workers, the property may need to be within walking distance of their work. The tenant may not have vast amounts of money, so the property needs to be clean but possibly basis, and the rent will be at the lower range. The property for a professional tenant will be the priciest, but will produce the top rent. The more pricey the property, the higher the rent will generate. This property requires high maintenance and offers high standard of décor. It's possible that it will have a garage or parking space, and possibly a security entrance system. The property for a semi-professional tenant is fairly different and slightly up-market. It can be close to transport links which go to the businesses, or financial centre of the local town. It's possible that the property will produce an average rental.

4. <u>Multiple sharers</u>

These properties will clearly be bigger and divided up in some way for either many unconnected people, or maybe for a large group of connected people, such as students or even nurses. In this situation, the property needs to be tough as it will suffer heavy usage. It will need to be located near to the university or campus or hospital, so near to where the potential tenants live. In both situations of students and nurses, the property needs to be very local to get back and forth regularly and on foot, and possibly at odd times of the day or night.

5.   Corporate lets

This scheme started off as being the only opportunity mostly in London, but is spreading towards many other big cities within the UK. This happens often when companies rent properties generally for their senior executives. They are generally paid or guaranteed by the company and the tenancies may be for long periods. Also, they are very responsible and reliable tenancies and the rents are high, but the property needs to be of the highest quality and in prime location.

To furnish or not to furnish

Whatever furniture you provide at the beginning of the tenancy, and if it's included in the tenancy agreement, you need to continue to provide that same furniture and in the equivalent condition throughout the tenancy. If the tenant provides the furniture, then they must insure it, but if you provide the furniture, then you must insure it. Meanwhile, ensure you avoid overspending on the furniture, especially for students, as you usually have to replace most items at the expiration of the tenancy agreement anyway. The decision to whether to furnish or not, is influenced mostly from the type of tenancy you provide. So if you offer accommodation for people, you need to provide furniture. Accommodation is normally provided, such as, if you have student lets, or sharers, or corporate lets. In this situation, you have more opportunities of finding a tenant and receiving a decent rent as these groups of people usually lack their own furniture or prefers to furnish to their own taste and standards.

– Furnished;

This is providing all the furniture required for living in the property, but there are basis criteria for this definition, which is that the property covers the essential furniture to allow a tenant to eat, sleep, and wash within the property. If these criteria are satisfied then there is a specific tax allowance, basically 10% of the gross rental, given as a deduction against the income by the HMRC. You can hire the entire furniture contents of a property; and fortunately that hire charge is tax deductible too.

– Part furnished;

This is providing the curtains, carpets and generally the white goods, such as fridge, cooker and washing machine, but this means that the tenant needs only to provide what they need in addition to this. Thus, the tenants would need to supply the furniture to sleep on, to sit and tables to eat on. The advantage here is that it's clearly cheaper for you, when you set up the property, but this level of furnishing is unallowable for the 10% 'wear and tear' deduction from the HMRC.

Be cautious with the safety aspects of the furniture, because in all properties, you must be completely aware of all the safety issues, legislations and regulations. This information isn't in-depth, but simply some general pointers to the main areas. In all situations, pursue the advice of a professional appropriately and if in any doubt, pursue advice from a reputable letting agent, or Trading Standards office. The main safety points to consider and comply will be both the Furniture and Furnishings Regulations and Gas Safety Regulation. Although not legally enforced, every reputable landlord would make regular checks and keep details of the serial numbers on the electricity equipment, such as the appliances, sockets, cables and plugs, and the smoke detectors to protect their tenants.

MONTHLY CASH FLOW FORECAST

Item	Total	January	February	March	April	May	June	July	August
Receipts									
Wages									
Other									
Payments									
Transfers									
Loans									
Savings									
Cash point									
Cheques									
Bank charges									
Card									
Insurance									
Car									
Credit Card									
Mortgages									
Net cash flow									
Opening bank									
Closing bank									
Item	Total	January	February	March	April	May	June	July	August
Joint									
Receipts									

Item	Total	January	February	March	April	May	June	July	August
Wages									
Other									
Payments									
Transfers									
Loans									
Savings									
Cash point									
Cheques									
Bank charges									
Card									
Insurance									
Electricity									
Gas									
Mortgages									
Credit Cards									
Net cash flow									
Opening Balance									
Closing Balance									
Personal Savings									
Item	**Total**	January	February	March	April	May	June	July	August
Opening Balance									
Receipts									
Withdrawals									

Closing Balance									
Business Ltd									
Item	**Total**	January	February	March	April	May	June	July	August
Opening Balance									
Receipts									
Withdrawals									
Closing Balance									
Business Savings									
Item	**Total**	January	February	March	April	May	June	July	August
Opening Balance									
Receipts									
Withdrawals									
Closing Balance									
Properties Account									
Item	**Total**	January	February	March	April	May	June	July	August
Receipts									
Rents									
Fees									
Other									
Payments									
Mortgages									
Bills									
Fees									

Item	Total	January	February	March	April	May	June	July	August
Subscriptions									
Expenses									
Wages									
Net cash flow									
Opening Balance									
Closing Balance									
Properties Account Savings									
Item	**Total**	January	February	March	April	May	June	July	August
Opening Balance									
Receipts									
Withdrawals									
Closing Balance									
Credit Cards									
Item	**Total**	January	February	March	April	May	June	July	August
(Card type) _% - cash _% with credit limit of									
Opening Balance									
Receipts									
Payments									

	Total	January	February	March	April	May	June	July	August
Closing Balance									
Available Credit									
Credit limit-Closing Balance = Available Credit									
(Card type) __% - cash __% with credit limit of									
Opening Balance									
Receipts									
Payments									
Closing Balance									
Available Credit									
(Card type) __% - cash __% with credit limit of									
Opening Balance									
Receipts									
Payments									
Closing Balance									
Available Credit									
(Card type) __% - cash __% with credit limit of									
Opening Balance									
Receipts									
Payments									

Closing Balance								
Available Credit								
(Card type) __% - cash __% with credit limit of								
Opening Balance								
Receipts								
Payments								
Closing Balance								
Available Credit								
(Card type) __% - cash __% with credit limit of								
Opening Balance								
Receipts								
Payments								
Closing Balance								
Available Credit								
Total Outstanding								
Total Credit								
Total Cash position								
Total Cash Available								

Entity comparisons

There are several ways you can set up and manage the property business. Which one you choose will dictate what sort of records you have to keep and submit, your liability for the business's debts, and how you manage tax. It's not always about how much you make, it's also about how much you can save. Your main financial objective is to protect your assets from as much taxes as legally possible. By reducing tax liabilities you are left with more after tax income and can therefore build your wealth more quickly. Generally, if you want to buy and hold properties for the long term and reinvest the equity releases, then buying as an individual would make more sense as it's easier to get mortgages. Otherwise, if you want to trade properties for the short term, then a company structure may be more tax efficient.

Generally you either own assets personally (personal assets), through your business, (company assets) or within your pension scheme or within a Trust. One of the most important factors when considering how best to protect your assets is the structures used to own and control those assets. Deciding which are the best structure for your individual situation can depends on what your preferences, goals and objectives, but I would recommend discussing your needs with a tax consultant or accountant if in any doubt.

More information on the most accurate and latest rates Income Tax, National Insurance, Corporation Tax, Capital Gains Tax, Inheritance Tax and Stamp Taxes, visit http://www.hmrc.gov. uk/payinghmrc

To help decide what is best for you and your strategies, consider if:

1. Are you trading or investing?
2. Will you have to give personal guarantees?
3. Do you suffer double taxation on earnings?
4. Will the funding be more expensive?
5. Do you understand the legalities of a company?

Company:

If you set up your business as a limited company, it means it's a separate legal entity, where you are protected from its financial problems, but in exchange, there are restrictions on getting the money out and more onerous reporting requirements. It's also easier to arrange your finances to minimise tax with a limited company than with the common alternative of sole trading. If your business is a limited company, it is owned by its shareholders. Even if you are the only shareholder, the business's assets and liabilities are separate to yours. You need to account for its income and expenditure, and you pay corporation tax on the company's profits.

The pros

–   Your liability is limited to whatever money you put into the business.

–   You may be able to arrange tax advantages compared with being a sole trader. Such as, a limited company can also pay out profits in the form of dividends, which don't attract National Insurance contributions at present. Although there is extra tax to pay if you extract dividends, a company can be an extremely powerful tax shelter if you can afford to keep reinvesting profits for many years.

– It's easy to arrange to take money out of the company in a tax-efficient way and the company's assets are its own.

The cons

– There is more administration to carry out in terms of paperwork and filing. You likely to end up paying professionals like accountants to do this for you.

– There are legal obligations on directors, and you can be fined if you don't carry them out.

– There are some rules on withdrawing the money from the company.

Income tax

Owners of businesses set up as limited companies often pay themselves a low wage, and take money out of the company as dividends (as a way to minimise tax and NI payments). You have to pay income tax via PAYE on any salary you pay yourself. If you pay yourself a dividend (and in any case if you are a director of the company), you have to fill out an annual tax return.

National Insurance

By paying yourself a dividend (and a low salary), you can reduce your national insurance payments. NICs affect your entitlement to benefits, so don't avoid them altogether (and nor can you if your business is successful—you have to pay yourself at least the minimum wage, which will take you into NIC territory). Remember, you are an employee of your own company as a director.

VAT

As with any business, if your turnover is expected to exceed a certain amount which can change annually, you have to register for VAT. Therefore, VAT-registered companies have to charge the customers VAT (putting your prices up), but you can also reclaim VAT on things you buy (reducing your costs). All this means extra record keeping (although you could consider the flat rate vat scheme) Nevertheless, some people will see VAT-registered companies as more respectable.

Corporation tax

Your business pays corporation tax on its taxable profits. The rules for corporation tax are more complicated when you set up your business. But that aside, it's essentially based on the company's income less its costs, allowances, reliefs, deductions etc. Rates vary depending on your profits and Corporation tax can be complex. But whatever your situation, ensure you tell HMRC that the company is liable for corporation tax, and that you pay it and file the company's return on time.

It's generally easier to get an accountant to do all this for you.

Building a Company checklist:

1. Choose a unique company name
2. Register at Companies House
3. Submit your annual accounts and annual return each year to Companies House
4. Tell HMRC you will be liable for corporation tax
5. Pay tax and NI for any employees (including yourself—and you must comply with minimum wage legislation, even for yourself).
6. Get a business bank account for the company.
7. Get headed paper printed; making sure it includes your company registration number, address and a VAT number if applicable.
8. Choose a director (you if it's just your company—and ensure you understand your duties).
9. Apply for VAT registration if turnover is over a certain amount
10. Take out any relevant insurance (such as public liability or employer's cover).
11. Pay a dividend to shareholders (even if you are the sole person.).
12. Get permission or a licence from your local authority for certain types of business.
13. Get an accountant—you can do it yourself, but with corporation tax it's far simpler to use an accountant.

Partnership:

You can set yourself up as a standard partnership or as a limited liability partnership (LLP). This can be useful if you have plenty of time but struggle to raise funds, so you partner with someone who has plenty of funds but has little time to invest, or someone who has the necessary skills, such as good management and experience, whilst you have plenty of time to contribute and determination. A limited liability partnership (LLP) is similar to a normal partnership, but also offers reduced personal responsibility for business debts. More like a company, rather than a regular partnership, the LLP itself, not the individual members, is responsible for any debts (unless individual members have personally guaranteed a loan to the business).

The pros

- They are easier to set up and run than a limited company.
- If you opt for the LLP route, your liability is limited.

The cons

- The extra benefits of an LLP are offset by some extra duties. There are more forms to fill in, and some members will have to shoulder extra responsibility as the 'designated members'.
- If you a standard partnership, your liability is NOT limited—you can be pursued for the partnership's debts.
- Although the nominated member has responsibility for the Partnership Tax Return, all the members will

be jointly liable for any penalties that result from it being submitted late or incorrectly.

Partnership LLP checklist:

1. Send Companies House a completed and signed Incorporation Document—form LLIN01
2. Display your LLP's name on the outside of all its offices or other places of business
3. Display your LLP's name on all its business stationery, including letters, invoices, receipts and cheques
4. Show your LLP's place of registration, registered number and registered office address on all its business letters, order forms and electronic business communications
5. Check that you received a Certificate of Incorporation from Companies House
6. Inform HM Revenue & Customs (HMRC)
7. Send an annual tax return to HMRC
8. Send a set of accounts to Companies House every year
9. Send Companies House an annual return—form LLAR01—in order to keep your LLP's records up to date
10. Inform Companies House of any changes to your LLP's membership, the personal details of its members or the address of its registered office.

Sole Trader:

Being a sole trader is the easiest way to start a business, there are fewer reporting requirements than if you set up as a limited company, although you do have to register as self employed via the HMRC. And accounting is much easier; hence bills for accountants are lower.

The pros

—   You are your own boss. You make all the money and you make all the decisions.
—   Less form filling means you will spend less on accountants' bills.
—   You have the ability to raise capital either publicly or privately, to limit the personal liability of the officers and managers, and to limit risk to investors.

The cons

—   You are responsible for everything, including any debts the business runs up.
—   You have fewer options to minimise your tax bill. Such as, Sole traders face a higher rate of income tax on net rental income, which can make capital repayment of borrowings seem expensive.
—   In some industries, you may not be treated as seriously as a limited company.
—   The business may slow down to a halt if you become ill.

Sole Trader checklist:

1.   Register as self employed with HMRC.
2.   Get a bank account so you can keep your business income and spending separate.
3.   Keep records of your income and spending (keep all the paperwork, and record it in a spread sheet)

4. Submit an annual tax return each year.
5. Pay class 2 and class 4 National Insurance Contributions (NICs).
6. Decide on a name for your company (if you don't want to trade as just your own name)
7. Get business cards, headed paper etc printed.
8. Think about using an accountant (especially if you employing staff who you need to pay PAYE for).
9. Register for VAT if your turnover is expected to be over a certain amount.
10. Get permission or a licence from your local authority for certain types of business.
11. Take out any relevant insurance (EG public liability insurance or employer's liability cover).

Trust:

There are many types of Trusts for different objectives. There are three parties in a living trust, namely the founder, the trustees and the beneficiaries. The trust is managed by the trustees for the benefit of the beneficiaries, and the trustees may also be beneficiaries. The beneficiaries can be any legal person, including living people, other trusts, and registered businesses. The founder may be a trustee and a beneficiary, although it is to be checked for legal precaution. The trustee may be either be a person or a legal entity such as a company. A trust may have one or multiple trustees. A trustee has many rights and responsibilities; these vary from trust to trust depending on the type of the trust.

The type of assets owned and depending on your objectives determines the type of Trust needed to ensure compliance with current tax statutes, but relevant lawyers and tax consultants can help explain in detail to what's best for your individual situation.

This involves careful planning and, in some cases, restructuring the existing business framework in a more tax efficient manner. Hundreds of the UK's biggest companies increasingly employ tax structures to limit the tax amount by adopting a number of sophisticated tax strategies to benefit from perfectly legal corporate tax mitigations. According to the National Audit Office, in 2006 more than 60% of Britain's 700 biggest companies paid less than £10m corporation tax, and 30% paid nothing at all by using a number of sophisticated tax strategies to reduce tax with perfectly legal corporate tax mitigations.

The pros

- Reduce your company's corporation tax bill.
- Reduce your personal income tax bill, whether you are a sole trader, partner, or self employed.
- Protect existing assets, (personal or company) from creditors, divorce or Inheritance Tax.
- Utilise existing pension funds for maximum benefit.
- Wealth management and planning
- Inheritance Tax planning, tax mitigation, specialised pension arrangements
- Pay the minimum amount of tax by law.
- Full control and limited liabilities

The cons

- Very costly and time-consuming to set up, but can be financially worthwhile if you have assets value over a certain amount to protect.

- You need specialist financial advisors who specialise in wealth management and planning, asset protection, Inheritance Tax planning, and tax mitigation to set it up for you.

There are many types of trust that exists for different types of circumstances, but I will show an illustration of how a 'Business Assets Trust' strategy works, so you have some clarification of its process.

1. As an Individual, you own shares in the 'UK Company'.

2. Within the 'UK Company', where you input tax free gifts of cash profits into the 'Corporate Capital Trust' (Resident Offshore).

3. Within the 'Corporate Capital Trust', you have a delegation agreement of investment powers to the 'Offshore Finance Company'.

4. Within the 'Offshore Finance Company' which is owned and controlled by trustees who have a Fiduciary services agreement towards the 'Nominee Company'.

5. Within the 'Nominee Company' which is authorised only to hold and receive funds for the offshore trust, but the funds don't belong to this company. It has a UK bank account. Normally the Corporation Tax, Income or Capital Gains is legally avoidable.

6. As an Individual, you own 100% of the shares in the 'Nominee Company'.

This strategy can be ideal if you have a property portfolio of residential, commercial or a mixture, and it can be mortgaged or owned outright. If you wish to obtain any amount in funds as the individual, you can 'borrow' the funds without any requirements from the Nominee Company, but it must be repaid back into your company with minimal interest. This legally disallows the HMRC to charge you anything, because it's treated as borrowed money (loan). You can convert an asset into cash, by selling it via this strategy without Capital Gains, VAT and Stamp Duty and reinvest the cash back into your company tax free. The trustees may only be professional people such as bankers, lawyers or accountants appointed by you, and it may be unlikely to appoint any related members of your family. Overall, it's vital to discuss with a specialist tax accountant or lawyer about what is the best options for your situation.

Acquiring and Improving credit

How your credit is judged

Your current and past credit record which can be tracked by agencies, from credit cards you have applied for and received, and reflecting the promptness of your payments. Store cards, car loans, home financing or renting, phone and electric bills, and mobile phone accounts can all be variables. Lenders want to see stability for where you live, with the job, prompt payments of past debt and a low debt-to-income ratio are also major determining factors. There are two major categories: one that is driven by factors other than financial and one strictly based upon income and debt. It usually takes a couple of weeks before any improvement is shown on your credit.

Most people automatically assume that the credit is the most important factor, but many lenders, including financial institutions, use what is normally referred to as the six 'Cs' of credit. They are listed here in the order of implied importance.

1. Credit: Your credit history
2. Capability: The ability to pay off the debt, based upon earnings and outstanding debt
3. Collateral: Is security required for the loan?
4. Conditions: Are there economic or regulatory influences that would come into play?
5. Capital: Your net worth determined by a financial statement.
6. Character: Does the person appear to be trustworthy? This is a summary of what is thought about you as a person.

The 28% / 36% Calculate Rule

The other commonly used credit rule to determine how much credit or mortgage a consumer can qualify for is the 28%/36% rule. This credit rule is used primarily by bankers and mortgage brokers. For standard mortgage programs, most lenders qualify your total housing expenses (principal, interest, taxes and insurance) equal 28% of their gross income. You take your gross monthly income, multiply the amount by 28%, and the resulting figure is the maximum amount one can afford for a monthly mortgage payment. The 36% refers to the maximum amount of debt versus gross income traditional lenders find acceptable. For those with very good credit, they may go as high as 38%. Car payments, instalment loan payments with more than 10 remaining payments, average monthly credit and score card payments, student loans, and alimony or child support payments fall into this category. So to illustrate, if your monthly income is £1,000, the highest monthly mortgage payment you would qualify for would be £280. Using the same monthly gross income, the total additional monthly debt allowable would be £80, or a combined £360. But some lenders/credit agencies may use a different calculation of affordability; you should seek advice from the lender or broker.

There is a difference between a credit report and a credit score, because a credit report is a summary of various accounts, past and present, opened in your name, including credit cards, bank credit lines, mortgages, store charge cards, and other bills, though usually not rent payments or utilities. A credit report will also include any collection actions taken against you, and any information of public record that may exist, such as CCJ, IVA or bankruptcy proceedings. On the other hand, your credit score is when you apply for a loan through a mortgage bank or other lender; they request your credit report from one of the three major agencies, who then calculate your credit score. Since your credit report might differ among the various agencies, your scores might differ as well.

Remember while the firm will not tell you why you how they measure the factors or points, they are legally required to tell you why you were rejected for credit, if that is the case. Also remember, that different firms use different factors, so if you are rejected at one, the next might not use the same method and you could receive a positive score.

Your basis and complete credit report can be more accessible, transparent and manageable by obtaining it from numerous online sources for free or for a small fee, thanks to the internet, consumer pressure, and even government regulation.

<u>A few of the numerous ways to acquire credit</u>

The key to building wealth is to use borrowed money or credit only for those items that will increase in value or appreciate, never for items that will depreciate like cars, gadgets, etc. Take your borrowed money and convert it into something that will go up in value, such as real estate. Then take the profits from that investment and pay cash for more assets that appreciate and you will find yourself on the road to building wealth. Building wealth is not any one thing you do right, but the total of all the little things you do right. And how you handle your credit will be a major part in determining whether you succeed or not. Obtaining, increasing and maintaining your credit are just one part of competent financial planning. The more you know about protecting your finances and assets, planning for the future, and spreading wisely, the more financially secure you become.

But using credit cards to fund investment can be filled with danger, because credit cards are for short-term borrowing and need to be managed carefully. Don't miss or be late with a payment, otherwise this will damage your financial health as well as your emotional one. Ensure you put in place safeguards such as Direct Debit Mandates for minimum payments.

A few of the many new and changing ways to acquire finances are:

> Personal loan:

Personal loans are often more popular than other sources of finance such as credit cards and overdrafts, because the amount you can borrow is typically greater. There is a high level of competition amongst lenders, which usually makes it possible for you to negotiate a cheaper interest rate than the one which you are initially quoted. By shopping around and negotiating a loan rate, you should be able to find a rate far more favourable than you are currently paying the credit card company. Loans are a relatively fast way to obtain funds for a special purchase or project, and even large amounts can be borrowed for almost any purpose. They are suitable for expensive purchases that require immediate payment, allowing you to spread the cost of the purchase and manage your short term finances more easily, especially if your loan has a fixed interest rate.

> ### Credit cards:

When starting out and you haven't had credit before, your limits are generally low, maybe up to £2,000 or so. Try to obtain a card that issues cheques. You may wish to bank a cheque for say £1,500. However don't spend it, but pay it back in one month's time when the statement comes in. You have just established the first steps into developing a credit history. You could purchase an item and return it before its 28 days return policy expiration, while it's still packaged with its receipts, to show activity on your credit card.

> ### Seeking a Guarantor:

One of the fastest ways to begin establishing a positive credit history and obtain finance is to obtain a loan by having someone else guarantee it for you. This works so well that I recommend applying for such a loan, by seeking out a relative or acquaintance that has good credit and ask that they act as a guarantor for you. Banks have no problems giving you a loan if they know there is someone with a good credit to back up the loan. If your friend or relative is a little anxious about risking their credit with you, tell them that you will even give them the proceeds from the loan so that they can pay it back. However, ensure that you are on record as having paid it back or it will not count towards your credit. Have them give you the monthly payments from the loan proceeds every month, add the minimal finance charge, and you should both be financially protected.

> ➢ Life insurance policy:

Some people have investment life insurance policies they have been paying on for years. Policies may offer a loan provision whereby you can actually borrow money based on the current value of the policy. This is often an overlooked source of funds that can be turned into an investment.

> ➢ Partners:

There are those who have the money, but don't have the expertise or time to hunt for and invest in real estate. More than likely they will be professionals like doctors, solicitors, accountants, etc. Contact any of them, explain how you could both make some profits, and see if they will partner with you. You do all the work, they put up the money, and you spilt the profits at a prearranged percentage. You always have the arrangement in legal writing to protect yourself and the business partner.

> ➢ Equity credit:

If you presently own your own home or another property, chances are you have built up equity in the property that you can borrow against. It's one of the easiest types of loans to obtain. Many financial planners caution against this approach and I share their concern if you don't know how to invest it properly. Use the money to purchase an income-producing property that will pay for it-self and cover the cost of the equity loan payments each month.

➢ <u>Home improvement loans:</u>

One of the fastest ways to increase funds when investing is through the use of one of the home improvement loans that are available. Put together inventories of all the repairs that are needed. Have subcontractors come in and give you a quotation for each type of repair. Then put them on a proposal form that you can obtain at any office supply store under your own contracting firm's name, mark them up 100% and submit it to the bank for approval. It's legal to be your own contractor for any property you own and no license is required. Just ensure that you do as much as possible of the work yourself. The more you do, the more you make. Best of all, the money or profit is not taxable income, because it comes from loan proceeds and your tenants will pay it off in time.

How you can improve your credit rating

You need to review the credit files in details. Go over each negative item and write down the story behind what happened. Of course, errors are usually the easiest items to remove, but it's possible and very common to remove factual negative information. That is why you need to inspect in detail anything that needs updating, correcting and confirmed with proofs. If you are married, ensure your spouse requests his or her credit reports as well. Some items might appear jointly while others could be reported individually. It's much easier to do both at the same time

Though the credit reporting agencies and credit agencies do make a sincere effort to maintain a high level of accuracy, mistakes can and do occur. Think about the volume of consumer financial transactions that occur in this country every day, automobile, home and credit card purchases, consumer loans, insurance, lawsuits, and so on. Credit reporting agencies gather the details on literally hundreds of thousands of transactions every day, input the data into the appropriate file and store it in the credit agency's massive computer system. Obviously, the potential for error due to the sheer volume of the clerical work is tremendous. There is another reason why understanding and verifying your credit can be so important.

You don't need a lot of credit cards to establish credit, just show an ability to be good at managing the repayment schedule. One of the many ways to improve credit rating is:

> Using a Store credit cad:

Your purpose is to establish a credit history, so choose one of the larger retail chains who will regularly report to the credit agencies. Some who deal in the credit market advocate getting a consumer card such as Visa or MasterCard first and then look for a retail card. But if you have a major credit card, you don't need a retail card. Check the interest rate and if you have shopped around at all, you see that your major card will probably carry a much lower interest rate, so if you already have a major credit card, don't bother getting a retail card.

Step one: Obtain a department store credit card, or at least a regular visa or MasterCard that is not connected to your bank account as a debit card to use this 'system' to boost your credit score. Find out how much you have available on your current credit cards. Hopefully they are not all maxed out, because this really only works if you have available credit to use.

Step two: Go shop at the department stores that you have a credit card for and if you have got £400 available on your visa card; purchase something that will total up to approximately £350 worth of purchases, but you will need to have enough money to make that one month's minimum payment on your credit card available though. Use your store credit card for the store you are shopping at to pay. Buy something you don't want or need.

Step three: Read your receipts carefully, most stores require your register receipt to return merchandise; so you will keep your receipt in the bag, taped onto the box, in a file, etc. so that you will be able to find it to return your purchase to the store. Most stores have a 30 (or 60 day) return policy. Wait until about 5 days from the full 30 days; return the item/product on the 25th day (or 55th day depending on the store/policies) for a full refund of the purchase price. Remember, it takes 3-5 days for a payment to reach the credit card company. So, by this time you will have made your one month's minimum payment on your card; you will have shown that you are using your credit line, and then you will return the product/items for all of your money back and you will also apply that amount of money back onto your card to show that you are paying 'ahead'. So in essence, the stores will report to the credit agencies that you are using your card and not only making your minimum payment; but also paying ahead on your bills. The store does not report that you refunded your purchase to the credit bureaus and this is not illegal. This is a proven method to improve your credit score if you can stick to returning your purchases and applying that full amount back onto your card as though you are 'paying ahead' on your bill. You don't want to create more debt by keeping the stuff you buy. For a test run, get a copy of your credit report now; and then one again in 6 months for any improvement in your credit score.

CREDIT MANAGEMENT

It's essential to understand before starting any strategies relating to using credit cards in a swinging method, is to ensure that your credit rating can survive the process, if you are using credit cards of any type. If you are going to start on no money down strategies for property finance regarding credit, then you are personally responsible for your credit history and reporting, so always ensure you regularly update your credit situation with credit cards.

Whenever you are making an application for a personal loan, hire purchase, credit card or contract, it leaves a 'footprint' on your credit file. You need to ensure not to go charging in applying for 6 credit cards individually altogether, since this could appear strange on your credit file. Even if they were just credit checks rather than credit approvals, there are also companies who may refuse credit simply on a certain number of footprints on the file. Therefore, guard this problem when you apply for numerous mortgages. If you can get one lender to offer you a chunk of nine mortgages, this leaves a much healthier trail on your credit file, instead of applying for nine mortgages with nine different providers. An alternative option is to apply for a line of credit instead of specific mortgages. Therefore, apply for an example £200,000 for a maximum 6 properties, as one application, but check around and you will find mortgage providers can do this.

By enlisting and contacting a credit monitoring company such as Expedia, Noodle and various more, you can view your own credit file and how it is impacted by your financial behaviours. Some credit monitoring companies inform if a monthly small fee is charged, but some don't charge anything at all. If you are able to pay a little cost to acquire your own credit file, then in a few days you receive a complete information pack about you and your money. Alternatively, you can subscribe to an agency such as Checkmyfile, and they will send you regular credit file checks for an extra cost.

Plan in a six monthly review of your credit cards aiming to increase your limits and reduce interest rates, but obviously you shouldn't try to increase credit daily, If you have any strange or false in information on your file, it may get removed, even if there are some genuine 'black marks' on file, you can help yourself by explaining these in advance to credit providers.

When you see the information, you could understand how best to use the information and how to modify it. There are many things you can do with your credit history, including modifying it or improve it, so it's well worth checking this now and then inspect regularly for changes. It's worth checking all the companies when you first begin, because they provide slightly different information, and then simply use the one you prefer for on going checks.

You can enquire through your local citizens' advice bureau, or look for credit advisors on the internet; you should speak to a debt counsellor if you are in any doubt about credit.

Ask the financial providers "what would I have to do in order to get what I need?" if you get a no or blocking answer anytime, and often, the finance provider will tell you precisely what to do, so you get your own personal financial action plan.

When you enquire or contact your credit card providers, remember to ask the questions within **C.A.R.D.S** as a reminder:

- **C**redit limits (What is the credit limit? How can you increase it? How often can you increase it?)
- **A**nnual fee (Is there an annual fee? Can it be removed? Or reduce it?)
- **R**ate (What do you pay? Can you reduce?)
- **D**eals (Can you get the 0% deals? Any other special deals available? Is there currently a better deal for you?)
- **S**pecials (Can you get the new deal? Or the exclusive package?)

CREDIT CARD SYSTEM

Credit	Current			New			Difference		
Card	Credit limit	Interest rate	Annual fee	Credit Limit	Interest Rate	Annual fee	Credit limit	Interest rate	Annual fee
E.g. Visa	£5,000	18%	£20	£10,000	12%	£0	£5,000	6%	£20
	£	%	£	£	%	£	£	%	£
	£	%	£	£	%	£	£	%	£
	£	%	£	£	%	£	£	%	£
	£	%	£	£	%	£	£	%	£
	£	%	£	£	%	£	£	%	£
	£	%	£	£	%	£	£	%	£
	£	%	£	£	%	£	£	%	£
	£	%	£	£	%	£	£	%	£
	£	%	£	£	%	£	£	%	£
	£	%	£	£	%	£	£	%	£
	£	%	£	£	%	£	£	%	£
	£	%	£	£	%	£	£	%	£

This credit card system is designed to help you find the best deals on some of hundreds of different credit cards, and there is always something that exists and matches your financial situation and strategies, if you look carefully for them. So if you are in the market for a credit card, keep a few things in mind: Don't use just one of the sites in your search (you are comparison-shopping, so compare the compare-ers too), don't think checking off a couple of boxes is a substitute for reading the fine print and analysing the results, and don't forget to consider cards from local banks and credit unions as an alternative to the big issuers that tend to dominate these sites.

Improving your selling, letting and buying strength

As the economic market crisis continues, getting the best tenants for your buy to let home is more crucial than ever. But how do you go about it?

Whilst many landlords might benefit from the cost of falling mortgage rates, they will simultaneously find themselves faced with new problems as a result of the deepening downturn. As public sector cuts bite and the cost of living increases, many landlords are expecting to see an increase in the numbers of tenants in arrears, which can be minimised if you choose the best tenants that pay as expected and treat your property well. This prospect, alongside the lack of opportunity to sell is why it has become even more crucial for you to ensure that your tenants are reliable, trustworthy and, ultimately satisfied.

If you are a novice landlord with mortgaged properties, the consequences of not receiving a steady rental income stream could spell a devastating shortcut to mortgage arrears and even repossession. Such as, for portfolio landlords with, say 20 properties, if one tenant fails to pay it will be absorbed by the rest. But for smaller landlords with say just two buy to let properties, if one doesn't cough up, that is half of your rental income. Remember to minimise the risk of accepting the wrong tenants who pay inconsistently, by seeking references, which should incorporate a previous landlord and current employer, and carry out individual credit checks to ensure which tenants are the best at paying consistently. You or the letting agent can do this vital process.

- Is your property competitively priced amongst similar or overpriced?

Ensure you do some research by looking at leading property websites such as 'rightmove' and check out the average minimum and maximum prices for your type of property in the area via the local estate agents, so that you are advertising competitively.

- Is the supply and demand in the area for your type of property strong or weak?

Despite the occasional short term fluctuations in the property market, the long term is always up, thanks to necessary cause that demand is greater than supply. I would recommend holding your property in a weak market; otherwise you will risk selling it for less than it worth due to a weak demand for purchasing properties. The market will eventually stabilise and even grow enormously. The reasons is due to increasing divorce rates, easier immigration, changing social demographic trends, more people going to universities and the number of new homes being built are decreasing heavily. The UK is a popular island with increasing population and people living longer than ever but with limited space. A substantial portion of the countryside is Green Belt which is strictly protected from development yet the demand for somewhere to live will always continue. Basically, if you are struggling to sell the property, then it is likely that the rental market is stronger, but if you are struggling to rent it out, then again it is likely that the purchase market is stronger.

- Is it the lack or wrong methods of marketing?

If you are using a letting agency to find tenants on your behalf, ensure you select a company that has signed up to one of the big property websites like www.Rightmove.co.uk. If you just rely on the local newspaper, people moving to your area from further away are unlikely to even see your advert so you will be limiting your potential market.

- Is the property presented as a home, rather than just vacant?

Present the property with some soft furnishings like cushions, vases with flowers, dimmed lights, pictures with summery natures or flowers and rugs. These can all be retained with you when the property is officially sold or let to reuse in another property and the tenants or buyers will personalise the property to their own taste. Buyers and tenants are generally unable to visualise a property as a potential home if it doesn't look like a home.

- Does your property stand out as the most presentable in the street?

Set your property apart from the competition as the best property to get the best tenants, by ensuring your properties come up to scratch. These days, properties will not only need to be clean and freshly decorated, they will need new white goods and all the mod cons. Appeal to the broadest possible tastes. Magnolia walls is a safer choice, whereas orange is something people either love or hate.

IMPROVING YOUR BUYING STRENGTH

It is important to know where to find these motivated sellers, because there is intense competition from other investors in every market conditions. Therefore you need to stand out by ensuring your strong marketing message attracts the buyers to call and sell preferably to you. Understand the types and how there are plenty of motivated sellers everywhere that are willing to sell you properties at huge below market values.

- **Broken chain:** These sellers may be more motivated to sell quickly by discounting it, after their buyers pulled out a once or more times, which is a frustrating for them and are often willing to finally sell at a big discount to move on quickly.

- **Deceased estate:** These sellers may prefer to quickly unlock all the cash, instead of being burdened with maintaining or refurbishing the property due to inexperience of property investing or bad financial timing.

- **Divorce:** These sellers want to spilt the assets, save as much heartache and quickly move on, therefore they are willing to sell at discounts to minimise a messy divorce.

- **Cash-flow issue:** These sellers are normally business owners with cash flow problems to inject some cash into the business to save it.

- **Downsizing:** These sellers prefer to sell their property quickly by discounting it, instead of losing out or waiting on a dream property in a warmer climate abroad or a smaller home.

- **Undesirable or static sale:** These sellers may struggle to sell their property after many months waiting on the market, because they lack the finance and effort to refurbish it into a desirable property, but are ineligible for a mortgage in its current state. They will sell it at a discount to move on quickly and avoid the holding costs. Also some properties appear refurbished but nobody is interested, because the demand to purchase is static.

- **Repossession:** These sellers are at risk of repossession by their banks and are motivated to sell quickly at a huge discount to clear as much debts as possible and retain their credit record.

- **Emigrating:** These sellers may want to purchase a property overseas quickly, without wasting time, costs and hassles maintaining the property in the UK, therefore they are willing to sell at a discount to move sooner.

Estate Agents:

You may prefer to find these motivated sellers via the estate agents before feeling more confident to attract the sellers to come directly to you or speak to someone who represents lots of sellers, if you know where to find them and appeal to their needs. It is important to get on to the estate agent's shortlist before they put the properties up for sale, because they will call you first know first if it matches your criteria, with the likelihood you may purchase it quickly. Everyone wins in this situation, because the motivated seller can sell quickly by giving a big discount, the estate agent can save time, hassles, earn a commission quicker and you will be amongst the few to be contacted first to get a great deal. It is worth putting in the effort to build an honest and reliable relationship with the Estate agents, because the results will be worth it.

Let the Estate agent know that you are:

- You are a serious and prompt investor who won't mess the estate agent and the sellers around, unlike all the other timewasting and indecisive investors.
- You are able to seal the deal as quickly as possible, because you have money ready to invest with. If you are a cash buyer then let them know that.
- The Estate agent feels they are the boss, because they will appreciate you asking them to help you and they want to be recognised as the expert in their job.

Avoid asking the Estate agents for all the motivated sellers and anything that is discounted like most timewasting and indecisive investors do, because you need to be specific and have a criteria list, such as:

- Do you have any properties with more than one agent selling it? They will be more motivated to work for you, because they want to earn a commission before the other agent secures a buyer.

- Do you have any properties that are listed for rent but would consider selling it? Many property owners rent out the properties while they struggle to find a buyer.
- Do you have any empty properties?
- Do you have any properties that have been on the market for a long time?

It would be useful to arrange a viewing outside of normal Estate Agency working hours, so you could speak to the sellers directly, and arrange how you can guarantee them speed and certainty, then they will likely guarantee your ideal discount. Remember you still want to maintain an honest and professional relationship with the Estate Agents, so give them feedbacks about the deals you have accepted. Also if your offers have been refused by the sellers, then remind them that you are still interested, and follow up weekly until the sellers grow more motivated and decide to consider your offer.

Newspapers, property magazines, property selling websites:

Advertising exist and works well, otherwise nobody would be advertising every week, therefore some of the advertisers are companies and many are investors like you and it depends where you live in how much competition is looking for the same thing as you are. Don't feel discouraged and expect instant results the first time you decide to advertise, because you can do a better job than half of the competition who don't know exactly what to ask, are not prepared and fast enough to complete the deals. Mostly many investors lazily copy someone else's specific strategy without really understanding its full process, asking the wrong question, too slow to complete a deal and unsure of what to expect.

Keep your adverts displayed for a few months, be able to answer calls from potential motivated sellers at anytime, ask the right questions to fully understand the situation, the property and their needs, build a friendly relationship and move very quickly. The potential sellers are very unlikely to leave any messages if you are unavailable to answer, but you could hire someone to do this for you with some prepared questions. Remember, the person who offers the most money doesn't always get the properties, because it is also about the relationship you develop with the seller until your offer has been accepted. It is likely the seller has called some of the other advertisers; therefore you want to complete the deal quickly.

It is your task as a property investor to acquire the properties for less than its worth, by helping to solve their problems and quickly. Consider asking these questions to get the right information to help you arrange how to create a win/win deal for you and the motivated sellers, because you can assess if the deal matches your criteria or not within about 10 minutes:

- Name, contact details with landline and mobile numbers.
- The full address of the property for sale.
- If it is a freehold or leasehold, because you will want to know long is left on the leasehold and how the service charges is.
- Flat, terraced, detached or semi-detached or bungalow.
- How many bedrooms and bathrooms

- If it has a garage, extensions, central heating and double glazing.
- Any work such as new kitchen, bathroom or wiring been done by the seller
- What is the reasons for selling
- What they think the property is worth and the reason for the price
- The amounts of the mortgage and arrears or redemption penalties
- Any other investors shown interest in buying?
- How soon do they need to sell
- When is a convenience time to view the property?

Property Inspection Checklist

Bring along a pencil, notepad, camera, a torch and a binocular.

	Comments & things to fix (function & cosmetic)
Inside the property	
Sanitary	
WCs	
Basins	
Showers	
Baths	
Electrical:	
Supply	
Lighting	
Appliances	
Fittings	
Fire:	
Smoked alarms	
Fire extinguisher	
Fire blanket	
Gas safe registered boiler	
Central heating and hot water	
Boiler	
Radiators	
Pipework	
Hot water cylinder	
Joinery Inside:	
Doors	

Staircases	
Handrails	
Panels	
Internal Fabric:	
Walls	
Ceilings and floors	
Fire place:	
Type	
Surround	
Live	

Outside the property:	
Gardens	
Paths	
Drives	
Ponds	
Walls	
Gates	
Roof Covering/type	
Structure	
Insulation	
Guttering	
External walls	
Doors	
Door case	
Porch	
Windows	

Uncovering a Property's true worth

Name:	Date:	Note

Address & brief description of individual properties	Net Purchase Price (A)	Current Value (B)	Loan Owing (C)	Net Equity (B-C)	Monthly net income (D)	Operating cost (E)	Monthly Cash flow (D-E)
(A) Date Acquired:	£	£	£	£	£	£	£
(B) Date Acquired:	£	£	£	£	£	£	£
(C) Date Acquired:	£	£	£	£	£	£	£
(D) Date Acquired:	£	£	£	£	£	£	£
(E) Date Acquired:	£	£	£	£	£	£	£
(F) Date Acquired:	£	£	£	£	£	£	£
Total of all properties:	£	£	£	£	£	£	£

Calculating a Property LTV Ratio

Operating Expense Ratio Total income / Total expenses	Property A	Property B
Mortgage information		
Total Loan Amount	£	£
Type of loan		
Term of loan (months or years)		
Interest rate		
Down payment	£	£
Monthly payment	£	£
Purchase price	£	£
Closing costs	£	£
Equity	£	£
Total initial investment	£	£

Loan to value (loan amount / purchase cost)	£	£
Cap rate (Annual NOI / Price)	£	£
Cash-on-cash return Annual cash flow before tax (NOI/Down payment)	£	£
NOI means Net Operating Income. An example of calculating the ratio: £1,000 income / £500 expenses = 1:2 (50%) then the bigger consequent number equates to positive cash flow. Whereas if it is £500 income /£1,000 expenses = 1:0.5 then the bigger antecedent number equates to negative cash flow.		

Property Portfolio Assessment

As you review the numbers on your portfolio, start to think about the following questions honestly.

- What was your plan for each property when you bought it? (Did you actually have a plan?)

- Do you have any benchmarks or performance targets in terms of growth and income, to know how well your properties are performing?

- Has each property performed against your plan or expectations?

- Has each property met your expectations for growth to date?

- What are the realistic prospects for growth over the next 1-2 years?

- Has each property met your expectations for income to date? If not, then list how you can overcome that.

- What impact does the net cash flow (positive or negative) have on the profitability of your portfolio?

- How well are you protecting your portfolio from unexpected problems, such as avoidable taxes, void periods and market changes?

- What return (combined annual growth and net income) are you currently achieving on that equity?

- What actions (if any) are you taking to maximise the potential returns from your portfolio?

- What is your 'exit strategy' for each property? In other words, at what price and under what circumstances would you actually sell? (Note: "Never" is an unrealistic answer)

- Is your equity working hard and getting you the maximum return on your money, or is it getting fat, lazy, or slow?

- If you don't have any investment property (yet) then just work out your starting position:

- How much cash do you have saved?

- What is the worth of any other (non-property) investment assets (e.g. shares) that you own?

- How much equity do you have in your home? (if you own your principal place of residence)

- Can you increase your monthly savings by minimising the unnecessary expenses?

- Have you discussed with possible investors about benefiting from lending you funds?

- Have you arranged with a Mentor to show you numerous ways to acquire funds, regardless of your situation?

Overall Property Assessment

Goal: Date of Assessment:	A: Excellent C: Average, E: Poor, N/A: Not Applicable Rating:			
Description	**Property A**	**Property B**	**Property C**	**Property D**
<u>**General & Street Appeal**</u>: How appealing does the property appear in general when compared to others in the same street and also the immediate vicinity?				
<u>**Comparative Sales**</u>: Research comparative sales for similar properties in same and neighbouring suburbs. Rate the strength in price growth over the past 12 months.				
<u>**Cosmetic Condition:**</u> What is the general exterior and interior condition of the property? Look for cosmetic defects that detract from the appeal of the property. Consider vegetation.				
<u>**Structural Condition:**</u> Locate and rate any structural defects that detract from the appeal of the property.				
<u>**House Layout:**</u> How well is the home serviced in terms of bedrooms, bathrooms living areas, floor plan, positioning on block, natural and artificial lighting?				
<u>**Land Size:**</u> How big is the land allotment? Compare land size in m² to other blocks in the same area. Factor in land usability like access, irregular blocks etc.				

Car Parking: How well is the property serviced in its ability to provide appropriate parking? Consider off-street parking, security, electric roller doors etc.				
Overall Rating: Based on your answers and lower ratings, now provide an overall assessment for this property.				
Notes				

ACTIVITY PLANNING JOURNEY

This activity planning tool guides you how to achieve your goal in small stages; you can partly or completely amend this to your individual preferences. Its helps to display this on your wall with your dream pictured above it. This can help you constantly focus, set dates, monitor your progress, review any improvement and changes.

Weekly	Actions:	Tips
Step 1	• Buy an Activity journal to note & keep anything relevant. • Speak to your partner/family what you are planning to do, how you are willing to sacrifice to do it & ask for positive support. • Fill in the whole financial report in pencil. • Register for a credit report; note its current rating & the flaws. • Write down how you plan your life to be in 10 weeks onwards • Note any relevant questions & all the doubts you feel. • Set up your business entity • Develop a business plan	• Swap a small amount of your time daily spent on TV, pubs and shopping for some financial activities • You hear negativities and doubts, but you are stronger.

Step 2	• Save a desired target of minimum percentage on the 'Needless' expenses and replace a desired target amount on the 'Need' expenses for low-priced. • Register & attend the relevant property networks locally, the nearest cities & check online versions too. • Order 1 or more audio books about wealth & properties. • Decide on what your strategy will involve • Practise calculating & matching 5 deals to your strategy. • List a minimum 10 investors & property lenders from anywhere • Role play with your partner on negotiation win-win deals • Acquire additional mobile or fax line to receive replies to adverts • Call on a desired amount of ads weekly	• Increase your time on financial activities daily. • Keep all receipts into 2 separate envelopes of Need & Needless for a desired amount of months minimum. • Listen to the audio books while commuting to & from work, shops and friends/family.

Step 3	• Consider what your strategy will involve & how it will match your preferences. • Decide & analyse the 2 areas you invest in • Search & register for 3 or more different BMV Property companies online for updates of property deals. • Study & attend 3 Auctions brochures by post or printed. • Follow a desired number of property inspirations on Social apps for tips. • Practise calculating & matching 7 deals to your strategy. • Change & update your credit rating for improvement • Treat negotiations as if you are a committed buyer • Begin to build your databases • Look for seller-finance deals	• Increase your time on financial activities daily. • Increase your saving and replacing expenses targets by desired percentage target.

| Step 4 | • List as many questions & concerns as possible to ask lenders.
• Practise calculating & matching 9 deals to your strategy.
• Revise your financial report & update with progress
• Apply for 1 or more credit cards depending on your strategy.
• Study all your notes and absorb the information.
• Look for money partners
• Role play with partner on negotiation strategies
• Develop your education plan for continued growth
• Set up your office | • Increase your time on financial activities daily.
• Increase your saving and replacing expenses by a desired percentage target. |

| Step 5 | • Identify local sources of property being sold. Look in newspapers, property sections in publications, property websites, auctions, hire sourcing agents or company, etc
• Practice your property analysing and number crunching, if it fits into your strategy rules.
• Have you assembled a power team as soon as you can afford it, to help you?
• Practice property analysis
• Practice contracts for purchase
• Practice financial statement
• Build up your power team | — |
| Step 6 | • Have you arranged a mentor found at networks and certain websites to help you start and progress?
• Continue to build and monitor your credit report and score. | — |

Property investment tips

- Know how to financially read an investment to know if it will cost you or if it will benefit you, by recognising the differences between an asset and a liability.

- The more control you have over an investment, then the better it is for you to ensure it succeeds.

- Invest in time and education, because it's the financial education that makes you rich.

- Increase the value of the property to increase the rental income.

- To increase the net income, decrease the expenses and exploit its undeveloped potential.

- It's the management of the property that affects the profitability, such as, if you are a great manager, then you could manage an under performing investment to perform its best potential. However, if you are a bad manager, then all investment is likely to be managed badly, which minimises its profitability.

- If you are looking to where are the best places to invest and will become desirable, find out where people are moving to and any clues of a location flourishing?

- Never go against the property market, because you can't change the market, but you can adapt and change with the changing market.

- It's not always about how many properties you own, because you could have 10 properties that generate £1,000,000 annual rental cash flow, instead of 100 properties that generates the same annual rental total. It's the quality instead of the quantity of the investments that can make a difference on your property portfolio.

- To understand the world of property investment, study their vocabulary to think and act like a true investor.

- Set a minimum ROI target, so you can be more flexible with choices and financially safer.

- Adapt your perspective to see opportunities with your mind like an investor, instead of only with your eyes. For example, when the average person sees an empty land, he will see nothing, but an investor will see a land soon filled with plenty of opportunities, like building residential or commercial buildings to resell or rent out.

- It's not always about how much discount you can get, it's smarter to think how much you can potentially make, such as, instead of ONLY focusing on buying a property for £70,000 instead of the £100,000 asking price, can you assess how to exploit it's unseen potential to be worth £200,000 or even more? Therefore, it's not always about trying to cut the price, it's also about seeing its future value in an asset.

- Always ensure you are driving up the asset's growth rate in rental or value, rather than just holding it by hoping for time and the market to increase it.

- Get experience by starting small and with small affordable risks, until you are more prepared to take more risks and bigger deals, because experience and education makes you rich.

- Be careful when financially looking at a deal on paper, because what may sound profitable on paper may not appear as expected when you view the property and its location. If it sounds too good to be true, then have a look and ensure the expectations is guaranteed.

- If you lack something, such as the finance or a great credit report, but you have plenty of time and determination, you could partner with someone who has all the requirements you lack but lacks the time and commitment, to do deals together. But, keep both yourselves protected with legal agreements.

- Always try to be the insider instead of the outsider, to find out where all the great investments are new strategies, news of the property market and more.

- Find out as many of the property investors who are progressing successfully, so you can study their moves and how they invest. To be the best, you must think and perform like the best.

- Timing can make a huge difference between profit and loss, because if you are too late, then you can't rewind time. But if you are too soon, then you still have a chance to make a success. So, know what clues to look out for, to know when the opportunities are coming.

- You can usually get a higher return on your money, when you use other people money, which is the beauty of positive leverage.

- As there is always countless opportunities everywhere and constantly when you see with your mind, then money will eventually attract to it like magnet, if you see how and know where you can make money.

- You should always make your money when you buy, instead of when you sell.

- Sheer persistence will always make the difference between you succeeding or not.

Property Investment advice links

- For directory, networking, property sourcing, finance, legal tips, landlord help and relevant contacts for property investing by checking out www.mypropertypowerteam.co.uk & www.yourpropertynetwork.co.uk.

- Contact the Land registry on www.landregisteronline.gov.uk. This site has details of over 19 million houses in England and Wales, it will give you access to the register on 80% of the homes in the UK with a minimum of just £3 fee.

- The site called www.myouseprice.com which has a fee of £1 for each property that you need data for (with a minimum order value of £2) however you can get access to data of recent property sales within 1 km of your home for free.

- For all kinds of statistical analysis, information and property prices for sophisticated investors, the site www.hometrack.co.uk provides all this for a fee of £14.95 + VAT per property.

- House Prices and property valuation data—including local area guides with house price/earnings ratio can also be found by checking out www.mouseprice.com

- A property and house prices website that provides information such as sold/rented property prices and current value estimates can be found by checking out www.zoopla.co.uk

- For information on local crime mapping, this site will provide that www.maps.police.uk

- To find out market value of rent or sale price of a property on over a million properties from estate agents and developers by checking out www.rightmove.co.uk

- For renting out your spare room tax-free up to £4,250 per year advertise by checking out www.homelet.co.uk

- For Landlord insurances, tenancy insurances and tenant reference checks by checking out www.housepals.co.uk

- To know about the local sold prices and letting price of properties close to your investment property by checking out www.nethouseprices.com

- Information on which disadvantaged areas is exempt from Stamp Duty by checking out wwwhmrc.gov.uk/so/disadvantaged.htm

- Information on the area's Education potential to attract family tenants by checking out www.ofsted.gov.uk

- Information on the area's environment such as flooding risks by checking out www.enviroment-agency.gov.uk

- Guarantees the title to registered land in England and Wales and holds records for land ownership and interests by checking out www.landreg.gov.uk

- For UK renovation and repossessed property auction listings by checking out www.propertyenquires.com

- For accurate and comprehensive commercial property research by checking out www.egi.co.uk

- For repossessions, developments, auctions, renovations, BMV properties mainly in London by checking out www.capitalpropertylist.co.uk

- To acquire a repossessed property directly from sellers by checking out www.repossessionangels.com

- For repossessed houses for sale, auction dates, directory by checking out www.repossessedhousesforsale.co.uk

- A directory of the UK's leading estate agents and letting agents available anywhere by checking out www.vebra.com

- For residential commercial properties to rent out or develop in the UK or overseas by checking out www.propertyworld.co.uk

- UK Repossessed, BMV, residential, commercials, lands and more by checking out www.cottons.co.uk

- For information and advice on starting a business, raising finance, government grants and loans, managing staff and related subjects for your property portfolio by checking out www.smallbusiness.co.uk

- For information on setting up a business and more by checking out www.bizhelp24.co.uk

- For information and advice on setting up and managing a business by checking out ww.businesslink.gov.uk

- For one of the most popular provider of property investments, property deals, tools and advice by checking out www.tycoonsystem.co.uk

- For the right documents, advice and everything to help you with letting by checking out www.landlordzone.co.uk and www.propertyinvestmentproject.co.uk

Terminology defined

Advance—another name for a mortgage or loan

Adverse credit—a loan offered to someone with a poor credit record such as mortgage arrears or county court judgements (CCJ

Arrangement fee—a fee for setting up your loan

ASU—accident, sickness and unemployment insurance, which covers your monthly mortgage repayments should you fall ill or be made redundant.

Base rate—the rate of interest set by the Bank of England. Sometimes lenders call their own standard variable rate their base rate or basis rate.

Building Report—a detailed survey of the property, this is recommended for older or more unusual properties.

CCJ—County court judgement, and is handed out for non-repayment of a debt.

Credit check/Score—the way some lenders assess the risk of taking you on as a borrower, based on your financial record and income.

Disbursements—the name for the various costs a solicitor will pass on to you when carrying out your legal work.

Early redemption—a penalty sometimes charged by a lender when you repay the mortgage earlier than expected.

Early Performance certificate (EPC)—included in a HIP and gives details of the energy efficiency of a home.

Exchange of contracts—the point at which a vendor's and buyer's solicitor swaps contracts and begin to finalise the purchase.

Freehold—land or property which is owned in infinity, as opposed to leasehold, where the owner buys the right to live there for the length of the leasehold agreement.

Guarantor—someone who agrees to guarantee your loan, and is fully liable for its repayment should you default.

Homebuyer's Report—More basis than the building report, it includes a valuation and should reveal any faults the property has.

IFA—An independent financial adviser who considers the whole market to find you a suitable mortgage.

Leasehold—gives you the right to occupy the property on the land that the freeholder owns for a specified duration.

LIBOR—London interbank offered rate, and this is the rate at which banks nationally borrow funds from other banks.

LTV—loan to value. The proportion of the value or the price of the property, whichever is the lower, that the lender is willing to offer you.

Negative equity—It's where the size of the loan on the property, is greater than the property's market value.

Remortgaging—arranging a new mortgage on your home, without moving.

Self-certification—where you declare your income to the lender, rather than providing accounts or payslips.

Stamp duty—a type of government tax on the purchase price of the property. This has been abolished for purchases in designated areas.

Title deeds—legal documents for a property valuation and it's an inspection carried out by a representative of the lender to establish if the property is good security for the proposed loan.